The Lost Notebooks

By Shari V. DeCastro

authorHOUSE®

AuthorHouse™ LLC
1663 Liberty Drive
Bloomington, IN 47403
www.authorhouse.com
Phone: 1-800-839-8640

Published by AuthorHouse 11/15/2013

ISBN: 978-1-4918-2538-9 (sc)
ISBN: 978-1-4918-2537-2 (hc)
ISBN: 978-1-4918-2546-4 (e)

Library of Congress Control Number: 2013918080

Thank You

First, I want to thank God for blessing me with a gift that I am able to use every day. He has given me a powerful outlet to free myself with and hopefully this can be a tool to inspire the world. I want to give thanks to all my love ones that inspire and support my talent. I would not have been able to get through this process without all of you. A special thanks to Jaclyn Bond for taking the time out to edit the images for this book. Last but not least, I want to give a big thank you to Kevin Rakeen White for believing in me and opening up my eyes to an additional path in life. This book would not have been written without your guidance. This book is dedicated to all the people that took the time to listen and read my words.

Today, it is a blessing to be able to share this with you. Thank you!

Table of Contents

Preface

In AD 3013 a young girl wandered off on foot, leaving the new world behind her. Curiosity and change fueled her strength to walk through the old county the elders called Kings. There were no signs of life—just broken land with rusty, abandoned buildings.

She walked toward the neo-Gothic style bridge overlooking the East River until she came to an underground pathway. She walked down debris-filled, black steps labeled "A/C." She quickly lit a match to clear her murky vision. Her curiosity led her through a dark tunnel filled with paintings she could describe only as colorful bubble writings. She frowned, trying to decipher the interlocking letters. After this discovery, her interest was at an all-time high.

She tripped in mid-stride. Stunned, she moved the match over a black-and-white composition book she had seen in abandoned textbooks. She flipped through pages and pages of blue and black writings and then put the book down. She walked forward a few steps and found three more books. She thought it would be great to bring back to the new world.

She ran back and picked up the first book she found. When her hands held all four books, her fingers started to shake while sparks of light and fire surrounded her. Oddly, she was not scared. In fact, she felt at peace, as if this was what she had waited for all her life. This was an internal transformation that had been destined since her birth. She was POWERFUL. She was PROLIFIC. She was a POET.

The Lover
The Storyteller
The Advocate
The Thinker

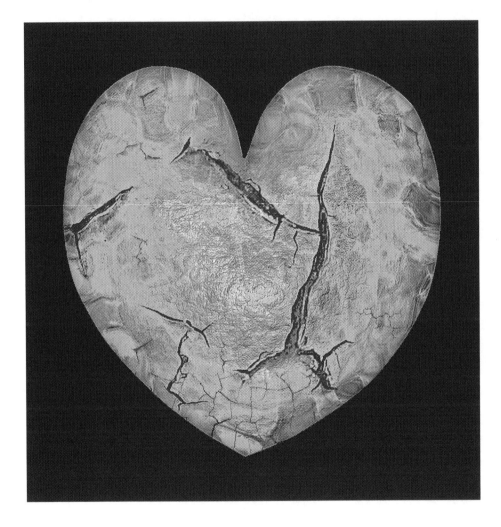

The Lover

As I sat in the dark tunnel, I was suffocated with an emotion. It was inviting and encouraging, with flickers of sadness. My right hand brushed a ballpoint tool that was stabbed into the dirt. I pulled it out and stared at the thin sculpture. I had an idea what this instrument was used for a century ago but I was not fully confident. What I did know for certain was this feeling—this strong feeling that I was compelled to write about. I opened the first used notebook to see an unusual detail. The entire notebook was filled except the first page. Was this page for me? I did not question it; I just wrote . . .

I love Love. It is my state of mind, the feeling in my heart, the attitude I breathe, and the principles I live by. As beings, we all know Love has different meanings and magnitudes. However, Love is survival. It is the pure instinct that all creatures have to function. We need it to preserve life and to fight against factors deterring its permanence. That is why I love Love.

We spend our entire lives craving, searching, experiencing, and nurturing Love. It magnifies our senses and heals our spirit. We live for Love, but we will die for it as well. Love is a vague phenomenon that can fulfill our lives and also be our destruction. The ambiguity of it can deceive the mind and can transform into corrupt behaviors and thoughts.

All creatures pursue a degree of Love without knowing if they will obtain the quantity. These expectations consume the soul, and the outcome may not reach its full aspiration. Love is tricky because the lack of it may be a mere distortion of our perception. That is why Love is so *fascinating and essential to our being, and the irony of Love is that it is still a mystery. It is our biggest motivation in life, and our pursuit of it dies with us. That yearning for that intimacy, that passion, and that commitment is why I am THE LOVER.*

Sappy Love Poems

I fucking hate sappy love poems
Not because they aren't good (believe me, there are
    some good ones)
But because they're fake
A faux pretense of want we want love to be
As I get older, love is not all glitz and gold
It's more of a motivating struggle that somehow
    touches the entire world
It's moving
But I still don't want to fall in love—I want to stand in it
Positioned intimacy
A situated reliance based on totality
See, love is already an unworldly phenomenon we
    humans overuse and underrate
To the point where love becomes artless
Like color without an instinctive perception
I know I'm getting all poetic on you
But, really, why do I want to fall into anything
Let alone fall into love?
I don't even like falling asleep without telling myself,
"Okay, close your eyes."
I keep trying, buuuuut that shit never works out
See, sleep might be the cousin to death, but love is the
    mother to life
And if life's a bitch, I guess love is a . . . cunt
(Sigh) in a good way though
Nah, but love mothers our existences, and it gets
    abused daily by the fear of unmasking the true self
So we get all bougee and Hollywood on love
    and overcompensate it with kisses, gifts, and
    misunderstood sayings like . . .
It was love at first sight
Really . . . was it really?
In the dictionary that clearly falls under lust
How could you love someone at sight but can't love
    yourself after years
At least take a third and fourth look

Or what about "Love is never having to say you're
   sorry"
Whaaaat . . . what does that mean?
No, seriously, what does it mean?
Every time I think I reach a conclusion, I am right
   back where I started
Or my favorite "You complete me"
Bullshit, Jerry Maguire bullshit
If a guy ever told me that, I would say
"Go fuck yourself"
And I mean that literally, because maybe then you
   will spend some time with yourself and get to know
   your attributes better, instead of benefitting from
   my qualities,
Because, trust me, I have some good ones
But, seriously, we know if we are not complete; love
   is a mere façade we try to be in and cling on to
   someone else to make sense of a life we have no
   control of
And I'm guilty of that myself
That's why I don't want to be in love; I want to be it
I want to embody emotion at its core
To open my senses to the unnatural
A fairytale that's told through eyes and is opened with
   arms
Because love is beauty and a beast
It just has to be contained and controlled through
   attractive honesty
See, I want the love story without a happy ending,
   because there is no ending
That's love
And I know this is sounding like another sappy love
   poem
But fuck it, because this isn't your typical sappy love
   poem
This is the truth

The Lone Soldier's Daughter

My mom taught me that home is where ya heart is at
But I never got attached, 'cause all I saw was my
    father's back
So now I give my back to the detached world
Because that man wasn't man enough to raise his girl
        Yeah, the lone solider with this deep internal
            pain
        Walks around with an X on his heart and his
            head down in shame
        A man running away from his responsibilities
        A man with an empty soul but possess great
            qualities
        That's why I never got it, and now love I don't
            show it
        That's why I became this magnificent poet
        That tries her hardest to look at the glass as half
            full
        Because half of my life is empty 'cause of the
            lone soldier's bull
        My parents were off-track 'cause my dad was
            racing at a different level
        And it's now that I realize I grew up behind
            schedule
        The hugs, kisses, and I miss yous were all delayed
        I know it's not all his fault, but he is still an
            issue
        So I press play on my radio instead of getting a
            tissue
        I flick through rap songs to teach me his insight
        Nas told me, "Life's a bitch," and I found out he
            was right
        The bitching in my life came from him
So when I call life a bitch, I'm talking about him
People don't take me seriously 'cause I'm talking out of
    anger
Yeah, obviously, but I mean every word; shit, he's a
    stranger

I don't know what he feels, but I know how to make a
    SongCry
I don't know where he lives, but I know the world is
    mine
I don't know his number, but I know all 36 chambers
He never told me about guys, but I know Ike, so I stay
    away from strangers
He never told me about sex, but I heard about Brenda
And he never told me about the government, but I
    heard propaganda
When I got my heart broken, he wasn't there, but I
    heard Ex-Factor
He was never there, but I heard the best medicine for
    it was laughter
So I cry my tears into radios for a shoulder
And my hate just grows for him as the world gets
    colder
Because I hold on to rage for days with no calls
No figure of a man when I look down the hall
The inconsequential sorry that left me with scars
So the only memory of a dad is through these bars
That I play over and over in my ears
To somehow alleviate the strength of my fears
To the point I think they are rapping to me and only me
And unconsciously believe that I'm their rightful seed
That's the pain from a fatherless daughter with rap as
    her guardian
And in her heart can give a fuck where her father's
    been
So I play some CDs when I have some questions
Put my headphones and take notes when I need a
    lesson
Those notes turn into my poetry I write religiously
They guide me to write with my mystical hands so
    indignantly
So when you see me zoned out for hours with
    headphones, I'm getting enlighten'
I can't talk back to them, but that's why I start writin'
Of all the things I never heard or felt from my dad

Yes, the Lone Soldier is walking around with a spirit
that's sad
His eyes are searching but his heart is stuck on
roam
Never finding the real value of home
So he walks for years, trying to find his way
While my idea of home is pressing play

Because of him I never believed that blood is thicker
than water
The striking complex of the Lone soldier's daughter

Five Senses

I carry the taste of you in the pocket of my clutch
And after I swallow it I can't help but blush
See, I wish every time I leave, I could take it to go
Unfortunately I just have to talk about it through this
    flow
But don't worry; I'll savor your flavor every minute
    I get
Just thinking about it now makes my mouth sweat
Regret . . . that I can't get a sample of you right now
So all I see in a blur vision is brown
Skin, I can't wait to touch
Rub lick, suck—sorry to be blunt
But having you is never enough
So I have to put my hands in cold water to even up
My hands get so warm from the close friction
People always said, Can't take the heat, get out the
    kitchen
So I rather stay in the bedroom and secretly stare
Envisioning your sculpture. How can this be fair?
Perfection in the eyes of an obsessive-compulsive
    spectator
When I'm with you, try not to blink so I can think
    about you later
Matter of fact, with your shaving cream I'll paint you
    on my forehead
Take a picture of you with my words before bed
I might seem neurotic, and maybe I am, a little
Infatuated with you and your middle
Maybe not a little, because I smell your cologne
On my pillow, press my face and I'm stoned
Your smell is addictive; I'm hungover from the sheets
Slurring the words you clandestinely said into me
It's cliché but hearing your voice is like serenity
And your love and affect is in the center of me
That's why I grip my stomach when you're gone
My thighs tingle with anticipation from waiting too
    long
Because I want to feel your vernacular on my private

While I'm in public I cross my legs 'cause I can't hide it
I still fight it, the urge to thrust my own skin
'Cause that would be cheating on you then
I really would be cheating myself out, honestly
'Cause I can't do half of what you do on me
Mentally without you I can't explode biologically
'Cause my emotions and passion intersects with my
     ideology
To know that anyone could move my heart and my
     being but only you do
So I turn my head to guys; they're jealous 'cause they
     can't be you
I'm selfish because I want to embody all your time and
     space
But I know physically that's impossible, but in your
     heart I have a place
I'll faithfully pay a mental fee just for you to subsist
     with me
At the address of my soul, you will always have the
     correct key
You can unlocked it anytime, any place, as you unlock
     my senses
I constantly Taste, Touch, See, Smell, and Hear your
     essence
Sometimes I get overwhelmed by the ability to
     experience you
No one can carry out the techniques the way I do
I am a liberal thinker and a conservative perfectionist
You are a willing transformer and a steady realist
So our beings together has led to hatred's exodus
We're not conventional, but that is where our progress is
I would say that we are perfect, but that would be a lie
We collide to make the infallible connection I can feel
     with my eye
The aromatic voice I hear with my nose,
The deafening skin I taste with my ears
The succulent frame I see with my mouth
The whiff of realness I smell with my hands
Shit, I can't help but to experience the five senses of my
     man

Dear John Letter

I remember the day you went absent
Repeating the events in my head like it just happened
Because I never wanted to forget
And it's easier to remember than to regret
Apparently you shouldn't live ya life with them
But what if you regret living life with regrets, what
    then?
I question that with black-and-blue bruises on my
    body
So I talk to my mind because I can't talk to nobody
I can but it comes with a lot of explaining and
    judgments
So I let the scattered memories of you stay on my
    conscience
The traces of your blotchy characteristics live in my
    reflection
I've forced myself to think of other matters, but you
    are the subject of attention
Consistently, every day, every moment, almost every
    breath
This is not a romantic novel, just a nonfiction piece of
    when my love left
The excuses to my neglect became paper-thin literally
So when you vanished, your physical absence limited me
I couldn't really think straight, and my thoughts
    curved into nonentities
Realizing, no matter what people say, you were the
    one meant for me
So I would jot words down, hoping you would draw
    your way up the tracks
But my emotional boundaries weren't outlined enough
    to get you back
So I tried mentally, but the telepathy method never
    succeeded
Thought transference could have worked if my design
    for you was completed
I concentrated on you but my thoughts never went too
    steep

Because your significance in my life was more than
   words; it was deep
You saved me and you understand the individual
   behind the face
So flirting with the thought and picking you up wasn't
   a waste
In fact, I liked the chase, begging for your number
   every chance I got
You told me, "Forget your number because letters get
   you hot"
So I studied the dictionary and impressed you with
   vocab
A lyrical genius so they say; Don't mean to brag
But those expressive terminologies had you wrapped
   around my fingers
And I got pain marks at the tips where your spirit still
   lingers
So I'm here with a bouquet of syllables and thoughts
   ready
The extrasensory experiences in my palms are well
   and steady
So those regrets in my life is mostly when I lost you
   way back when
I'm regaining confidence, picking you up and writing,
   Dear Pen

Real Conversation

Why can't I have a real conversation?
Why can't a boy give me some mental stimulation?
Is that so hard to ask for nowadays?
I guess so, because your hard stick is the only thing in
    my way
If you dare try to think with that shit, I'll make it
    bleed
Don't fret. I'll have regrets, because I do have needs
But please, can we talk for a second?
Can we sex through words so I can learn a lesson
Like where you came from and where you're going?
And maybe later I won't mind if your thing start
    showing
But what happen to the simplicity of questions I used
    to love
Little but strong questions that gave conversations a
    little shove
Like what's your favorite color? Mine is blue
What about you? Let me guess—blue too
Yeah, it was questions like that that made it all
    worthwhile
And to think we thought being simple was going out of
    style
Like who's your favorite artist and what's your
    favorite song or album?
Pac, It Was Written, and Sam Cooke's "A Change Is
    Gonna Come" is one
Something old but new in my heart
Favorite books are Invisible Man and Malcolm X—was
    hooked from the start
A strong man with a plan is my type of guy
And if you heard I write, it wasn't a lie
But writing is my life, not a pastime
So when you hear my phrases, it's more than a rhyme
It's more than a sport, but basketball is my favorite one
My favorite tools are the pen and the gun
I make magic with one and relate to the other
A form of protection—never had a big brother

I'm not violent, just by any means necessary—feel me
I talk softly but speak in volumes more like Huey P.
But anyway my favorite drink is ice tea and my
     favorite soda is Sprite
I love to dance, laugh, analyze, and of course write
My favorite place is my bed, where I sleep and write
     rhymes
I want to go to Africa, Greece, Haiti in my lifetime
My faith right now is something I'm studying and
     trying to accept
Oh, and my favorite movies are Coming to America
     and X.
You see, it's more than a line to open my thighs
But it takes one empowering line to open my eyes
See, before sex I want to know your dreams and fears
What's been keeping you motivated for all these years?
Me, being a poet 'cause I spent sleepless nights chasing
     my dream
So failure would be the biggest downfall to my poetry
     scheme
And with my soul in the mix a lot is at stake
I have to admit I'm terrified of snakes
I'm not even joking, I really am
What? You want to know what I look for in a man?
Well, one, he has to be intelligent; he can't be
     anywhere close to dumb
I mean, since he has a dick, I don't want him acting
     like one
Two, he has to have a sense of humor, 'cause I can be
     sarcastic as shit
And if he can't take the heat, it will damper the
     chemistry a bit
Three, he has to share a passion for words and music
     like I
Since I don't smoke, I need someone to roll my loose-
     leaf so I can get high
I need them to live through the bars so they can relate
     to me
So they can see why I'm trying to create this dream
And, hey, maybe that person was right

When she said I'm looking for a Nas, Malcolm, and
  Einstein in one
Sounds pretty farfetched, but my search ain't done
But this isn't about me; it's about knowing someone
  deeply
Your stick won't get far, but my knowledge of you is key
If we connect through our minds, I can feel you
  sexually
This is just something that been bugging me
As I get older and more mature
So is a nice stimulating conversation so hard to ask
  for?

The Wake-Up Call

I want him here with me
Because his time and space gives me life
When he's gone
His spirit is withdrawn from my heart
And every beat . . . beat . . . beat is in agony
This is selfish of me to want him right now . . . I know
But myself isn't a self without himself
So in actuality I'm self-less
I'm human but I'm not a being without him
So I sit up in this queen-size bed
And contemplate . . .
Should I wake him up right now?
I'm bored but mostly lonely
And he would cure that in a single second
With a "good morning" or a "hey, Babe"
Aaahhh, wouldn't that be nice?
But all I hear is deep, rhythmic breathing
That I only like to hear when I'm sleeping myself
(so I don't have to hear it)
But the one good thing about this is
I get to watch him at peace
Without any worries
Without any fears
Without any expectations
He is safe
Without the world sticking up its middle finger up at
    him
I get to watch him be happy
For a few minutes without any interruptions
And I get to smell an aura of harmony within his body
It's almost magical watching his chest go slowly up
    and down
Like his body is laughing about this unworldly joke
    unheard
And his feet twitching with excitement for the next
    dream
So for a minute I'm content that he is content
In a content of rigid silence

So in this moment it would be selfish of me to want
*   him right now . . . I know*
But once that moment is over
I contemplate . . .
Umm, how should I wake him up?
Should I do the two hands on the torso shake
Or quick smacks on the back
Or the "accidental" stretch of my arms to his face
Or the romantic, kiss-on-the-lips greeting?
Honestly, I can't bear to physically wake him up from
*   his serenity*
Because I can watch him like this forever, literally and
*   figuratively*
The calmness of his soul gives me so much pleasure
So I smile at his still but inspiring state
And I finally decide to grab the remote and entertain
*   myself*
Until my king arrives
And as soon as I hit that power button
I feel his humanity pour out his eyes
And I hear "hey, Babe"
It works every time!

Emotional Evaporation

As we lie in a bed filled with emotion
Wrinkles left with spoken word
I put my head on your chest
And collapse into a world of thoughts
Facing the ghost of relationships past
And the premonitions of what's ahead of me
Thinking what is left to deal with
What other obstacle do I have to surmount?
To obtain this
To attain happiness
Internal tranquility
A sense of liberalism
With love and with life
What else will I have to sacrifice?
To obtain triumph over all the demons
We call problems, trust, and growth
Time, tears, pain, and stress was enough
So I close my eyes
And listen to the rhythm of your breathing
Striking the back of my neck
In a unremitting pattern
With the same breath that went inside of me
That said words that brought tears to my eyes
And the one that changed my heart and outlook on
    life
I tap my fingers to the rhythm of your inhalation of air
And the beat of your spiritually most fragile organ
Your heart, at the heart of your being
The substance that kept us together
Through all types of tribulations
Like anxiety, patience, and separation
I could hear the blood passing in and out
Through the missing pieces that I tore
Because of the abandonment
The missing moments in the memories
We were supposed to have
That didn't exist because of my fears
And my emotional withdrawal

That held us apart
But that also brought us closer
That made us partake in moments like this
With your finger traveling through my scalp
Like it was a subway map
Trying to find your destination
To where my inner thoughts reside
To feel the thoughts that keep my eyes open
During the end of the black sky to blue heavens
Hoping you were out of harm's reach
And only one call away
Instead of one shot or hit away from the hospital
Or one deal or trigger away from jail
As you spiritually touch the hippocampus part of my
    brain
Where I hold all my memories
You feel the abundance of sentiment
Having a mental picture of the times we fought
The times we laugh from cracking jokes
The times I cried alone because of anger and
    apprehension
The times I tried to make you envious
You smirked as you realize you did get jealous
All the breakups to makeups
The tension after all the hang-ups
The uneasiness I got to pick up the phone to call
The time you save me from hazard zone you call life
That made you pull back your wandering fingers
Because of the intensity that brought that memory
    back
To the scene of that moment
That made you feel guilty and embarrassed
And now I'm left with the traces of emotional
    touching
Sounds of blood rushing in and out your heart
And portions of your breath on my neck
And as I lie on your chest
My head descends down to the bed
My hands land on my covered mattress
The breathing on my neck is the stream of air

Coming out the vulnerable window
While I only hear the sounds of my heartbeats
And my sheets cling on my skin
And only my skin
There are no more wrinkles of spoken word
And the bed is filled with only one emotion
Sadness
My bed is lonely and cold
And the memory of you is that
A memory

Yo, I Heard You Like Hip-Hop?

Yo, I heard you like hip-hop?
Well, I got hip-hop written all over me
So let me spit some street poetry in ya ear, homie
I'm known as the hip-hop cheerleader who can get
    lyrical
I've been lingering in the soul of many artist
    materials
Trust I got Illmatic lines flowing through my veins
Doggy Style, too, 'cause Snoop smoked me thinking I
    was a mary jane
And when I can't stay restrained, I get a little Pac in me
When I want to spit some G lyrically, I use some Biggie
    in my poetry
If it were a game, I would be MVP on the P-A-G-E
I might have been late, but in '04 Big L put it on me
And artistically I got Lauren Hill's essence inside me
I've been sweating Rakim's technique for years; it's in
    my psyche
I got particles of Reasonable Doubt in my cells
And in a tribe called quest is where I dwell
So if you want to come over, I'll explain you the
    scenario
While I play Dead Prez's "Mind Sex" in the stereo
And we can talk about our beloved hip-hop
I have to admit, I'm feeling you a lot
And when we start talking I ain't tryin' to stop
Hoping our words will "break" the air as they pop lock
Together to form our chemistry
As you sit directly next to me
I'll write a poem glazing into your eyes
On that page is where my feelings will lie,
'Cause usually it's me, myself, and I like de la soul
But since I met you, my heart hasn't been cold
It's been open, and I need love like LL
Shit, I don't know what you do, but you doing it and
    doing it well
My umi says, "Shine your light on the world," but I
    rather shine it on you

Mos Def told me that, but I guess my umi will do
The point is, hip-hop ain't the same if we're not
    hearing it
And by the way I write, you can tell I'm the Lox—
    living off experience
I don't need money, power, or respect, just you
Okay, maybe respect and power too
But fuck the money, although I want the bread
I rather have the magnificent one like Special Ed
'Cause your love will always outweigh my wealth
Can't put a cost on the person who makes my heart
    melt
I have to say my life would be inadequate without you
    as my number one
So you would be my public enemy if we don't fight the
    power of love
I hope you take a relationship into consideration
Because we learn so much just through conversation
So imagine what we could have in store
With the five elements and so much more
And if you decide to tell me you love me, it would
    never be paper-thin,
'Cause that means our love transcends hip-hop, and
    there isn't a we without him

Sex, Love, and Videotape

At night I don't need to dream about you I think
    about you
All throughout the day, and yeah the night too
Dreams don't cut it, I mean, they're a part of my
    reality
But it's the memories I think about that gives you
    actuality
So I'm not writing this poem just as an ode to you
But because I feel deep in my internal spirit I'm
    supposed to
I have a need to throw out my ink-filled pencils and
    lead pens
Write with blood from my fingers so every word can
    come in tens
I'll put it in an envelope and ship it through e-mail so
    it can be everlasting
You and I could live for eternity through these poems
    I'm plastering
On subway doors, on laptop keys, and glasses of Ciroc
Love is addictive; I sip my words slow for you and take
    it on the rocks
Because the love is light as one, not like soap-opera
    anecdotes
They walk on clouds but we choose to walk down dead-
    end roads
There is realism in dead-end streets that can't be
    depicted on television
We can encounter roadblocks and decide to walk
    through the situation
When people walk on clouds, they just fall to their
    death
At least we could can see the issues and revive what's
    left
And I revive it in every cursive I stroke in my
    vocabulary craze
See this poem was written more as a symbol of our
    love then praise

Love may not last forever, but forever it will be
     organic
From all the secret tongues and special passwords that
     made it magic
See, to me, fighting for the remote is romantic
And I believe not only your touch but your rich
     thoughts are orgasmic
Most of all, your unreserved attitude has become a
     therapeutic tool
When I am in chaos your presence makes everything
     else seem minuscule
This is why I rather think of you then have some half-
     interpreted dream
That is a metaphor for something I don't get because of
     an underlying theme
My mental videotapes of us are adequate enough to
     watch through my mind
And instead of eating popcorn I'll just microwave
     these poetry lines
In reality, dreams aren't interesting if it does not come
     into effect
In actuality, life has a vivid freedom dreams can't
     accurately reflect
So I can lose some sleep for dreams that can't
     expressively duplicate
The Free Dome in my mind of sex, love, and videotape

Brooklyn

Last night I dreamt I was in Brooklyn again
I was back on my block looking ahead
Looking at the place where I grew up
Thinking about the times when I screwed up
Brooklyn, you was a part of me
I was the heart; you was my artery
All the memories we had were unforgettable
And our bond was just unbreakable
I tried to leave you so many times
To the point "I'm leaving" just became a line
There were times I thought I'd left
But in reality I didn't take a step
Because I was there through ups and downs
I stuck through the smiles and frowns
Through the hustle with money and drugs
Rustle with the NYPD and thugs
Brooklyn, just and only for you
And I would do more too
Because you was all I wanted
It was like my love was daunted
It was so overwhelming and intimidating
The fact we wouldn't let go had to be premeditated
Because even through the menacing and crimes
Through the court dates, sentences, and time
I was there for you, Brooklyn
And I never went looking
For another place to rest
'Cause that would be losing a lot less
Although sometimes I didn't agree with that
'Cause you wouldn't get off my back
Yeah, I probably went through a couple of boroughs
But, Brooklyn, you kept it more thorough
You were real, gritty, and at the same time sweet
Not like Harlem, Bronx, the Island, or Queens
And all the late nights in the streets
That made my poetry deep
Made me more responsible and mature
But at the same time immaculate and pure

That made me the woman I am now
I guess that's why I stuck around
You taught me how to struggle
You got me into trouble
You showed me heartbreak
Helped me get over my rape
Made me laugh and cry
Made me tell you the truth and lie
Made me feel special and neglected
You made me curse you out when I meant it
Made me pour out my feelings and emotions
Left me alone when I was just hoping
To be with you and only you
You made me feel blue
You made me feel intolerant and patient
You showed me severance and relations
You taught me to hold on and never let go
You taught me how to write and flow
You brought out the poet in me
You showed me how to breathe easy
And showed me how to breathe hard from stress
You left me in pain and restless
You showed me affection
And gave me protection
That's what Brooklyn meant to me
So it's sad that I have to dream
About Brooklyn that was so true
Because Brooklyn was you

So So Sorry . . .

I have too much pride to say I let tears fall
Ignore the pain, there are no feelings involved
That's what I tell myself some days
Or I drink the clear or dark to clear the dark away
'Cause for the first time I really let myself down
Now when I'm alone, there's no fake joking around
It's real life, real hurt
And some people think I'm a fucking expert
The fucking expert that don't take her own advice
Afraid to say I should have thought twice
Or a third
And now I'm ashamed because I can't write a word
It's not you; it's my fault I lost my own talent
I'm the reason why my thoughts went stagnant
And I can't believe I'm the reason that you're not here
I lost my voice in the process because I cared
To be honest, I'm not even sure which one I'm talking to
Because, sad to say, there was more than one of you
That's the first time; it was hard to admit it—
Keeping that in, can't believe I wasn't admitted
And I'm sorry
So so sorry
That I let you down and I let you go
I should have been there to let us grow
And if God forgives me and lets you come back
I'll try my hardest to fix the mishaps
I will be that person you needed the first time
And this is a real testament, disregard the rhyme
This is the only way I know how to express my true
    emotions
I want to live again without the mental commotion
So this is for you and for me
And now we can be together through my poetry
Gone but never forgotten lyrically
And maybe now I can stand the image of me
I finally gave my heartache life
I was drowning slowly in a world pool of strife
The agony took a life of its own without my consent

Now I can write and breathe at your expense
I hope this apology is not too late
Because the fact I heard those words today was fate
So today my denial washed away with the cries
And when I say I love you, it's not a lie
You and I know my real truth
My real feelings that now I can finally live through
This is a personal oath that was well overdue
And in your honor I won't say this poem was about you
'Cause I'm sorry
So so sorry

Release Your Heart

Release your heart
Expose your eyes
And completely disrobe your mind
Leave them nude and unprotected
And uncover your ears to my words without any
    poetic predisposition
Because I want your mind to get the feeling of blissful
    knowledge
That you can't learn but you can visualize
Through my almond eyes
And observe the attraction I see, that I could only
    describe as
RED—
The longest wavelength discerned by human sight
Because your aura makes heat emerge up to your
    pupils
To create rose-tinted tears
Then your body becomes a stained canvas
Where I'll write out your heart
So release and expose your spirit
Just to me
Because I understand your liveliness
It's like the energy of the sky during sunset
The moment between day and night
When life is timeless.
And time will hold between your lips
While love escapes to your soul as you kiss me
Passion unleashes control and leaves vulnerability at
    its climax
A magnetic connection that was predetermined
The day God drew his image of us
So please release and expose your mind
Strip down to your deepest thoughts
So I can plunge into your humanity
That body I see is an illusion
So the world won't get to know you like I know you.
And when I get to that innermost point,
I will cure your beliefs with my voice

I'll do that for you
All you have to do is release and expose your eyes
Untie them from the negativity and bias you seen
Forget about it for one second, and I'll make it last
    forever
If you let me
Because concealed in your eyes is the essence of your
    being
And I'll hold it with the strength of gravity
I'll even protect it with them closed
Because eyes can see life more clearly sometimes in
    shade
Just release and expose your ears
Loosen each vibration
And let go of the world's chatter
So I can run my fingers through your blood
That flows thirstily to refresh your mind
After you hear me
Savor my words as I listen to your breath
So I can move with the rhythm of your core.
The distinct moment when human nature becomes
    tangible
All you have to do is release and expose yourself
Because your experience is a metaphor but is felt as a
    simile.
Yes, insightful but yet a little eccentric
At times it can be complicated but when understood
Your spirit is simplicity at its best
Zip down to your uncertainty so you can have trust
    in me
And our love will be our sacred treaty
So as I said before
Release your heart
Expose your eyes
And completely disrobe your mind
Leave them nude and unprotected
And uncover your ears to my words without any
    poetic predisposition

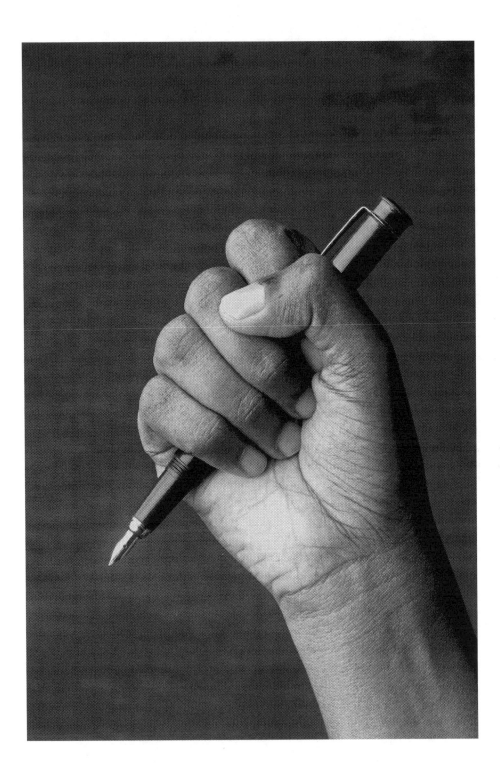

The Storyteller

I walked up the steps with the books in tow. I didn't realize how much time I'd spent down there. It felt like time had stopped. The sun would soon set, and I wanted to get back to the elders before it got too dark. I walked for miles. I was restless and barely could pick up my feet.

I tripped over a silver pole. It was labeled with a green sign "Flatbush Ave." I was so tired, I stayed on my knees to catch my breath. As I stayed in that position, I pulled out the ballpoint tool and drew a picture in the hollow dirt. I got up with a half grin and wiped the dust off my knees. My half grin turned wide open when I looked at my picture in shock. My drawn picture was in words. That's then I realized . . .

I was born to tell stories. I illustrate life with words by crafting pages of vivid encounters for a captivating relation. Storytelling is one of the deepest forms of connection between individuals. It's an emotional correspondence among narrator, character, and spectator. This connection forms a profound union, joining the past, present, and future. Storytellers analyze past experiences to influence future on goings. That is why storytelling is in our everyday lives. It is a prominent part of our society. It's in our music, television, movies, news, and books.

However, storytelling is not just for entertainment. It embodies our education, and it is the framework of our history. This art form paved the wave for our present world. Before written words, it was oral communication that led to the building blocks of society. As a storyteller, my drive is to tell not only my truth but the world's truth. I do not want to just teach; I want to inspire the mind to learn. I want to birth understanding through a distinct picture of creativity.

It is amazing that words can evolve into a physical entity that people can feel and think about. I give out knowledge but leave room for the spectator to interpret. Stories are a tactful strategy to enrich the mind, and they change the way people see life. That's why stories will continue to discreetly lay out the construction of the future. Hundreds of years from now, when these pages are gone, the words will still have meaning.

My purpose in life is to be seen and felt, and I fulfill that through words. See, everyone can tell a story, but there are a few that can become the story's vision. I am THE STORYTELLER.

Lost Miracle

Sean was a miracle, like a baby's birth
His personality surpassed any money he was worth
We met in class in the back of the first and second rows
He was intelligent like black thought, because it showed
That intimidated me, but made me better in an abstract sense
And every time he looked at me, my body got tense
I figured out they were just feelings circling my body
The way he treated my mind as a place and separated it from
    my body
And I was able to talk to him and make a mental stance
Because we became partners in a group project by chance
We started talking after class, making our plans
And it wasn't long after that when it led to romance
Not the sexual romance you're thinking about
But the kind that left me pondering in doubt
Like how this shit could be happening to me
When I was sitting at home alone while Lauryn was rapping
    to me
I lost focus in his love and design
I was locked in his mind like it was a crime
We spent as much time together as we could
Held hands while the other was balled in a fist as we stood
And everything was good . . . .

Yeah, until shit started to change to a stage like no other
It was like I was talking to another man, 'cause he was acting
    crazy like a mother
Yeah, Ima shut my mouth, 'cause I couldn't speak the truth
I was in denial and ignoring the clues
I couldn't see it, like I was sprayed with mace
That shit was right in my face
And everywhere we went he left a trace
So now I had to keep my eyes open to say my grace

It all started when I found the white stuff between the sheets
And in my mind I never would have thought he would cheat
So I gave him another chance so we could grow
But then he started doing some shady shit on the low

He started sneaking out at night to go to her house
And when he came back, his hugs left her scum on my blouse
He quit his job to take a week vacation with her
Thinking the whole time he ain't kiss me the way he kissed her
She took over his life; he didn't go to class anymore
He gave up everything and anything for that whore
I went to his crib, raging when I saw her hiding under his bed
I couldn't understand what she was doing to his head
To make him deceive me the way he did
How I could be with him after the lies he lived
Gazing into his teary eyes as he tried to kiss me with her shit on
    his lips
Looking at his pocket full of coins—bagging groceries for tips
This is his life that made him so closed in
Didn't you hear the song, how that girl is poison
With all her love marks on his arm?
He even gave that chick my grandmother's charm
She had him shaking for her love; he couldn't let her go
Thinking it was all good just a year ago
I guess I wasn't high enough for his love
Since that day he meant her in the bathroom at that club
And since then he just cannot get enough of her stuff
As the days passed, he crumbled and I lost trust
All he wanted in his heart was her; I couldn't take him back
'Cause that girl was poison, Carla, Christina—nah, crack

American Dreaming

He sits in a box in between New York City and New Jersey. He sits for hours, listening to old school jams as cars come and go. Hundreds of dollar bills touch his wrinkled hands—the same hands he used to walk to this country with thirty years ago. He's looking at the frail green paper he dreamed about for years. The sad part is that those bills aren't his. He's a hard-working man with a fucked-up psyche, because the land of opportunity screwed him over.

Back home he heard America had gold streets and trees of money. He dreamed of lying on plush soil and being mentally liberated. At home he was free but was trapped in the chaos of poverty and politics. So he worked day and night to escape the place he always called home, because it did not feel like home anymore.

As soon as he stepped on America's dirt, he was stamped an immigrant and a nigger. The only thing he knew was that he was a man that wanted a better life. Now he was faced with different mental struggles that fucked up his psyche. Some people say he asked for it—that it was his choice to come to the land of opportunity. But in his heart he had no choice, and now he chooses to smoke and drink the pain away. In the past he was a prominent lawyer, but today he says, 'Toll please . . . Have a nice day" a hundred times a day.

Not Your Typical Black Girl Lost

Her face is the inner-city backdrop
Heels walk where rats stand at bus stops
Her hands been cuffed by handcuffs, no cops
And her eyes seen so much her lenses have grim spots
Her body and mind is so distant
And when it comes to trust, she so [resistant]
Her heart been crushed and beaten down by bulldozers
And every time she tries to walk away, **shepullscloser**
See this isn't the typical story of a black girl lost
Because this is a story about a corporate boss
Living in her corporate world in her uptown penthouse
Sitting behind her Italian desk, watching HBO's *Cathouse*
She worked hard to reach the top, dealing with so much prejudice
But now she reaching for girls, wishing **Craig** had more **lists**
So she can have a rendezvous with one, maybe two
To conceal the guilt of her abortions—one, maybe few
Buried in her heart, she thinks that's what her mom shoulda
    done
Instead of leaving her at a McDonald's at the age of one
So Dad had to fend for himself—his salary for fixing cars
He was the best father he could be, besides the nights at bars
So happy she never caught her daddy's disease, being an alcoholic
She wasn't careful and got caught up being a shopaholic
Her eyes spends bigger than her Louie V wallet
And all her money washes down in her luxury faucet
So she is constantly at Chase bank chasing favors
You know addicts have multiple addictive behaviors
So she's paying for escorts and not paying attention to her debt
Oblivious she needs porn, 'cause humans barely get her wet
But the best part is her best friend she met at Lincoln HS, ninth
    period
Who been there throughout all her Lindsay/Britney periods
She helped her pay for college so she never had to **touch** a pole
Gave her places to live, never out in the cold
Nevertheless, she fucked her best friend's husband, a female
    Brutus
Funny, 'cause her husband with the nice Caesar was named
    Julius

36

The one man she ever truly **loved** wasn't even hers
Wasting nights trying to convince him to move to the 'burbs
But all he did was m o v e money out her account until she was
    bankrupt
Her face is filled with *humility* and abuse she can't cover with
    makeup
Spending her nights under the tunnel, lying with laymen
So calling her a black girl lost might be an _____
                                    Understatement

Brick Lady

Beautiful brick lady, please don't die
I know the war ain't over, so please don't cry
Many died fighting the war to paint over ya body
So I know they're in heaven, drawing on clouds, prolly

This kid asked me, "What is the meaning of struggle?"
Well, I saw a spray-painted name in a subway tunnel
And received some info on him to find out he was locked in prison
His graffiti walls became a four-block cell in the system
Since he wasn't getting paid for his works on street buildings
He got caught in the hustle doing street dealings
People told him to get a real job, 'cause the world gets cold
He told them he can't, 'cause graffiti art is in his soul
His money, his girl, and his art became his wife
Until his beautiful baby girl came into his life
But being a decent man doesn't always pay off
He was drawing a portrait of his little girl when he got caught
Drawing for hours to only end up in the precinct
During that time, a murder was done by a Puerto Rican
You know the saying, wrong place at the wrong time
Well, because of his look, he was put in a witness line
His face was accidentally picked as the criminal
When his only crime was using his hands as his visuals
The poor artist got a full life sentence
He wasn't good with grammar, but art was his profession
So he continued to draw as he served his time in the bin
And in New York his name began to ring
And traveled all around the world
With his most famous portrait of his little girl
Crying freedom out her little eyes
But the fame didn't stop time from passing by
Well, his heart got cold
Graffiti art got old
As his wife got stone
And his daughter got grown
So he read the daily news every day to get his mind off that
But nevertheless the thoughts almost always came back
His life and the news stories caused a wall full of pain

As he read an article about a Dominican family getting slain
"Damn" was the only thing he could really say
Thanking God his family was still safe for another day
And minutes later killed himself with the same hands that got
    him fame
'Cause his hands drew blood after he read his family's name

So the definition of struggle is life, 'cause that's what makes us cry
And the struggle only stops the day you die
So as you live, struggling, keep hustling to survive
'Cause death is never the solution to watery eyes

So beautiful brick lady, please don't die
I know the war ain't over, so please don't cry
Many died fighting the war to paint over ya body
So I know they're in heaven, drawing on clouds, prolly

Reverse

Out fuck the get . . . that's what I said
Infuriated and distressed as my eyes turned red
Any kind of relationship we had was dead
When I found pink draws that wasn't mine under the bed
This dickhead didn't know all the diseases he could of spread
Fucking these girls to maintain his street cred
Then my hand lifted off his face while his head turned back
To the position before as I decided to give him a smack
As he said, "You on cheat never I'll"
Saying the "Me wasn't it" bullshit with a smile
With my hands up, I asked whose panties are these in reverse
But as my hands went down, his reaction showed he had it
    rehearsed
Of course he would—he wasn't a foreigner to using charm
After he put his hands back in his pocket, proceeding open arms
"Baby, Hey," he said, walking back to the door with his keys
    jingling
And while he turned the locked, I sat back down on the couch
    trembling
I put my head in my hands as the tears dripped back up through
    my fingers
As the recent events in my mind lingered
Following the overturned lyrics to Nas's undying love in my
    stereo
I put my head back up, took the remote to put the volume to
    low,
Emerged from my couch and backpedaled to the phone
I said, "Shit," right before putting the receiver to my dome
To hear the voice of my home girl Laure
Cursing while I told her the backward story
Of what I found under my bed
After removing the phone from my head
I place it in front of me as I heard the dial tone
Pressed talk after searching for her number on my cell phone
Locked it, and put it in my pocket
And the house phone was back on the table like I dropped it
I decide to call my friend after throwing up the Ben & Jerry
As water rolled up to my eyes to make them teary

I put the ice cream back in the fridge and ran backward to the
   bedroom
And every backward step, the stress bloomed
Broken glass merged together back into a picture frame
A photo of us hugged up that was dropped in rage
Lifted up to the dresser
My breaths traveled back in my mouth, lowering my blood
   pressure
All my belongings I dropped went back into place
As the anger went into disbelief, changes on my face
I went back down on my knees to look for my shoes
When I encountered the substance for truth
"Fuck the what" is all I could say
To the piece of material that started the unforeseen accounts of
   the day

Hip-Hop Head, Part I

There's only one boy on my brain
(Yeah, I bet you talking about Dame)
Nah, I'm talking about Tyrone from May
He definitely dipped a drop of dawn dat day
His syllables shined on me so brightly
He walked on stage and gripped the mic so tightly
He had me mesmerized with verses, hooks, and ebonics
Imagining I was his student for a rap hooked on phonics
He was real hip-hop, and the crowd could not change him
But too bad a commercial act went and out staged him
The hurt in his eyes had hurt me mentally
I thought with that connection it was meant to be
He left me with a drop of his sweat on my palm
And a touch from when he accidentally brushed my arm
He made me feel so special like he was rapping to me
But it was just his drive 'cause he was rapping his dream
And when he walked off the stage, he walked out my life
But they say if it's destined, you'll see 'em twice
And it happened, when I went to a lyricist lounge
An emcee was rapping his lyrics and checking his sound
I turned and when he looked up, he cracked me a smile
He came over to me in disarray like he ran a mile
Asking me if I wanted to sign up tonight for the program
It wasn't him; it was just the sound-check man
I got my hopes up for no reason; I felt like a dunce
So I guess it wasn't destined 'cause I only saw him once

Hip-Hop Head, Part II

I thought the next one would be a gem
But I couldn't choose between them
It was like Pepsi or Coke
'Cause one was blood, the other was loc
And honestly I prefer Sprite
So that hip-hop head was just right
But I couldn't obey the thirst for him
And plus my crush got worse for him
I became obsessed with his lyrics in my dome
I was rapping it hard when I was in my zone
Like he was my own intimate, unsigned hype
Fuck that, he was an *illmatic* classic, five mics
He got five on his first time, no second thought
And I'll buy his shit no matter what the record cost
But instead of five mics, I'll give five kisses
For every punch line in his rap disses
But instead of kisses, sometimes I'll give him five daps
For the nigga P was talking about in live nigga rap
'Cause he exist in signals through the music
It's beautiful the way his voice and the beat just fuses
That's why I can't seem to block him out my mind
Because the sweat in my palm was a sign
I'm tired of thinking about him gripping the mic
I want him gripping me in the middle of the night
Rhyming through the wee hours in the night
Freestyling together would be in the right
But now I'm alone to face the stage
Feeling like the tranquil bird in the cage
I signed up to spit a piece of poetry
It feels good to feel that peace within me
But now that peace is erupting quickly
Because I couldn't express it lyrically
I always wanted to, but there was hesitation
That hip-hop head gave me some inspiration
So I decided to sign up for the program tonight
And I decided I was goin' choose two rhymes to recite
A conscience one and one for the love on my mind
It was time, and I was finally going for mine

So when I heard my name, I started my first rhyme
And I started stuttering on the first line
I was embarrassed and ran off as fast as I could
I shattered my spirit at the exact place he stood
So I sat on the floor in a corner, just crying
And I heard, "Everyone messes up. You're just trying."
He touched my shoulder and gave me words of wisdom
If I didn't look up that second I would have miss'em
The hand on my shoulder was the one on the mic
I held back a smile with all my might
And told him I couldn't spit after what happened
He said I just had to turn the laughter into clapping
How could I if my poise shattered in seconds?
He told me he would teach me his secret weapon
He said he prays before he spits a rhyme
And thinks of someone special before his first line
So it gave me the confidence to walk back
I took my time to get myself on track
A part of me wanted to run and give up quick
But I looked back, and he gave me a wink
I said a prayer and thought of someone unique
As he watched me the whole time, I felt elite
That night two dreams came true
I spoke my poetry and met the person that got me enthuse
I'm not going to lie, he never got to grip me like his mic
But I'll never forget the hip-hop head I met that night

No Signs Say Out

As she lies wide awake
Trying to ignore the heartache
By holding firmly on her pillow case
Facing the opposite direction of the empty space
Unfilled with her husband's presence
Who's been gone since eleven
The time that's almost noon but is still morning
But no matter what time, she still lives in mourning
Every time he closes the door
Because she does not see a man, just a whore
How can this be the man she fell in love with
When now she can't bear to touch him
But she does
Because she is still in love
With a man with no respect for his wife
Sleeping with women as a double life
Sneaking home late and kissing her on the cheek
Breaking her down week to week
And she can't bring it up with communication
Because he goes crazy, making it seem she is mistaken
But she knows she's 100 percent right
But she can't bear to fight
To lose an endless battle that ends at the beginning
With no possibility of her winning
So she bottles the pain, sadness, and rage
And lets it gradually escalate
To the point where she can't function properly
Her conscience and her heart has an inner rivalry
That she can't control
So every night she explodes
Into tears of disenchantment
'Cause years ago, if she knew, she would have left him
But to her it's already too late
She put in too much work to escape
So she tolerates the cheating
Because she can't bear to see him
Just walking out, leaving
'Cause he induced her with mental beatings

So now she can't accept losing him
So she withstands the abuse from him
Days go by with indications of less meaning
So she spends a lot of her hours dreaming
Of a life she thought she would have
With no thought of the future she could have
If she left her filthy husband
But she promised to love him
'Til death do them part
But the only thing dying is her heart
She doesn't understand the magnitude
Of what an abusive relationship can do
She lives with cold mornings and lonely nights
And hold onto the small amount of good memories tight
Not knowing when she will have a good one again
So she cries until her eyes turn red
So she stays awake in her emotional, water-filled bed
Listening to him say, "I love you" in her head

Dirty Harry

Chris from Long Island was the average guy
A good student and most knew him to be pretty shy
His dad was a doctor, but daddy was also a playa
The type of guy that fucked a prostitute without paying her
It was a thrill to smack her around, that feeling of power
To come home to a wife who been drinking vodka every half hour
He was a distressed man that lived an abusive life
Then took it out with abuse to his wife
And his daughter, Sara, with bruises on her back
But she was more consumed about being fat
She just wanted to be the girl in the magazine
But now her daily problem is costing her dream
She just wanted her face on Seventeen, but that's decease
Since the only place you see her face is on top of toilet seats
Then there was Chris, who stayed locked in his bedroom
Praying to God that he would be dead soon
Shaking every time the Suburban pulled up at his home
What happens when a kid can't escape the broken suburban
      zone?
Well, he leaves his family and the white-picket fence
So college became his escape and a quick defense
He had to leave that house of bad habits
Because the O'Donnells were and only will be addicts
No matter where he went his life and pain wouldn't deplete
And since the O'Donnell's are addicts, Chris became addicted to
      being a police
He joined the NYPD force back in '96
And was put on patrol in Brownsville around 96th
That was his favorite corner to harass little boys
Flashing his badge, stick, and gun like a toy
He was that policeman that brought corrupt into cop
He got hard seeing a bullet and busted when he fired a shot
It was a thrill to see these boys leaving the streets to jail
And it was always a good day when someone got life without
      bail
His mind was distorted with stereotypes and false statistics
That's why when he was at work, he was always suspicious
He believed that everyone was evil at their very nature

And if he couldn't make an arrest, he felt like a failure
He also spent his off days transporting drugs to the ghettos
The hood only an experiment filled with thugs and chicks with
    stilettos
The extortion turned the project bad, but that's what he lived for
Giving extra money to Mr. Ahmad to kill black brutes in the
    corner stores
He thought he was sacrificing himself and he was the street's
    savior
But he was only really doing it for his own favor
'Cause the memories he lived with killed his heart slowly
And the bloody cross he carried was the closest thing to being holy
Yeah, his chain that hanged on his neck with real bloodstains
The memory with clear reflection of pain
That lingers with him on his trigger finger and patrol car
And no matter where he goes, he can never go that far
From the home with the Suburban inside the white picket fence
That made him feel like he was always the victim on defense
See, the Suburban never left the driveway since he left home
He got tired of seeing that man called Dad plague his soul
It was one night when he had a bad dream, and he starting
    scheming
'Til he broke out his room when he heard his mom screaming
He silently opened his mom's room and let off a shot
That exact moment he decided to become a cop
Every cop has a little criminal in them to deal with one
And ever since that night his pure existence was undone
He was never the same after he killed his own daddy
That's why the streets ain't know who Chris was—because he
    was known by Dirty Harry

Doing Time

My dad died
Well, I mean he's not alive
He went away five years ago
So I'm crying through this flow
Tears can't drip anymore
Heart is ripped and torn
Up in pieces from the blood on the gun
And now my feelings are numb
So I let the blood drip instead of the tears
Cutting my arm to alleviate the pain for years
Watch the blood trickle like it did on my dad's hand
Can't talk to God because I don't trust no man
And Mom was never the same when her dad died
She could never be a good mom with money on her mind
To settle her desire through crack in her nose
Pretty on the eyes besides the bruises underneath her clothes
Slashes on her arm through injections
Tears on her face because she became society's rejection
People look away, people point, people laugh
But people don't know that makes her relapse
She quits every day and sniffs every night
So my little brother goes to school and fight
Ds and Fs are the only letters he knows in the alphabet
In the hallways making little girls panties wet
He spits on teachers and throws tantrums
But no one really wants to see where they're stemming from
They just see another thirteen-year-old delinquent
But through the fits and screams no one bothers to listen
To the fact Dad left but isn't a rolling stone
And Mom could be supportive if only she wasn't stoned
And I can't console him, 'cause I'm in my room cutting my body
While our uncle plays with little sis to commit sodomy
Yeah, she is only six, thinking touching pp is a game
So uncle drinks bottles of alcohol to diminish his shame
Little sis knows that every sip leads him into her room
So she tries to block the door with a wooden broom
And she tries every time, knowing it doesn't work
Praying it will stop him this time from lifting up her skirt

And one day he did stop lurking around
When Dad stopped by, coming from the halfway house uptown
Caught his brother doing a devastating act
Pulled a gun out, and never looked back
See Daddy didn't die; Daddy got life
Doing it as time, living it in strife
He didn't physically die, but he died out our lives
The distance makes him invisible from our minds
My uncle was a victim, and our family was a victim too
We can't visit, and we talk when calls get through
His soul is the only thing beyond the glass
And it's slowly dying from the occurrence of the past
See, my dad died but is still alive
While he's locked up, we all are doing time

Shattered Dreams

Shattered dreams of a love unreal
So imagine the pain this young thug feels
Gave his heart and soul to a woman who ain't care
Life's a bitch when you find out it ain't fair
Now he is battling between Cupid and the Devil
Taking the pain and agony to a higher level
Drinking and getting high to get over the stress
Thinking she still here rubbing on his chest
But the substance abuse got his brain possessed
Hearing the woman he loved repeatedly say yes
To a life that could never be
Who knew dreams could die so easily
Like a baby in her womb
But that dream along with others got locked away in a tomb
Buried under her lies, deceit, and abuse
With traces of her juices left on the beds of other dudes
He fell for the oldest trick in the book
Thou shall never trust a crook
'Cause the crook stole his heart
Broke it—and now he's a man apart
Separated from the world he living in
He thought his baby girl would stay faithful 'cause she a
    Christian
But there was something hidden behind the sign of the cross
Behind it was a black girl lost
Who left him with memories he wish he didn't have
Trust—it's a motherfucka when you can't erase ya past
That you wish you didn't live and regret
So what's left?
Nothing, but a house that ain't a home
Just a place to rest his dome
With shattered dreams of a love unreal
Shit, only he can imagine the pain he feels
He gave his heart and soul to a woman who didn't care
Who turned all his dreams into nightmares

Animation Domination

I had a dream that **Gabriel** was smoking a blunt with the **Devil**
And they tore up some Mickey Ds as their high settled
Cupid threw away his arrow to start shooting with a rifle
Saying a bitch is a bitch 'cause they're so fucking spiteful
So **Mother Nature** got her heart broken and became a whore
And from then on there weren't sunny days anymore . . .
Just black clouds and black rain in the cold that turned into
    black ice
So **Santa Claus** ran for president and became the black Christ
And there was no red-nose **Rudolph,** just a bull dog with a
    fucked-up leg
In the same town that **Big Bird** killed **Dr. Seuss** because he
    fucked mother hen
The Things videotaped the sex and lies under the Sesame Street bed
Big Bird knew it wasn't his kids, because **Mother Hen** laid green
    eggs
So in the morning **Big Bird** made green eggs and ham for **Betty
Boop,**
Always wanted to fuck her because he had dreams of fucking a
    prostitute
Betty Boop was tired of that life and choked her pimp to death
    with a trench coat
And at **Bugs Bunny**'s funeral **Porky Pig** ended his eulogy with
    "That's all, folks"
Bugs was real flashy, throwing his carrot gold at all the honeys
He should have known what would happen when he left a good
    bunny
Bugs dipped his honey bun in **Pooh Bear**'s honey jar
Curious George saw them monkeying around in **Roger Rabbit**'s
    car
And he told **Miss Piggy**, and everybody knows **Miss Piggy** has the
    biggest mouth
So **Pooh bear** overdosed on his honey before the whole town found
    out
By that time **Mickey Mouse** lost his movie deal with the **Mario
Brothers**
So **Bell** and **Cinderella** had to start hustling, because they're
    both single mothers

And **Minnie Mouse** was poor and alone and moved in with
 Garfield
But **Garfield** was a "dog" and cheated, so **Minnie Mouse** had to
 play the field
She dated **Odie** until he gave her fleas he caught from **Scooby-Doo**
So she became independent and started to teach at **Barney**'s
 school
But **Barney** got jumped by the **Teletubbies** gang run by **Elmo**
Barney was a pedophile; he was arrested by **Storm Elmo**'s main
 ho
See, **Storm** left **Superman** the day the **Jetsons** and **Flintstones**
 started a war
Superman lost his fame because **Batman** was the first to stop the
 big uproar
He moved back to Krypton and was remembered just as a "big
 Boy Scout"
And **Batman** was the hero, not because of a bam and pow; he
 just took a sneaky route
See, he stole the **Back to the Future** car with **Wonder Woman,**
 Wolverine's wife
And **Wolverine** dug his claws into the soil until **Captain Planet**
 came back to life
He died in a forest fire caused by **Smokey the Bear** smoking
 cigarettes
Who committed suicide because he couldn't live his life with deep
 regrets
Captain Planet didn't have regrets after he heard that the
 Back to the Future car wasn't a hybrid
He killed off everybody with earth, wind, water, and fire to save
 the entire planet
And he ended that day with "The power is not yours—only
 mine"

No, this is not the **Twilight Zone** or **Disneyland**; it's my mind
That's when I woke up from my imaginary dream, high off my
 bad habit
This is my mind on drugs, I have to admit. And I won't quit—the
 mind of a poetry addict

The Advocate

I continued to walk, tired, dehydrated, and slowly becoming delirious. In the midst of the night, I heard the sky call my name. I stopped dead in my tracks, looked up and around, and there was no one in sight. I stood there in shock, waiting for an answer. That is when I saw a barely standing wooden construction with "Cyclone" written in a tarnished red tint.

As I got closer, I saw a body of water ahead. I ran with enthusiasm, knowing soon I would be able to replenish my mind and body. After becoming hydrated, I fell asleep right on the cool night sand.

I woke up to hearing my name like it was pronounced by the waves of the ocean. I was sane, and I could not understand why this did not seem bizarre. It was a calling of some sort. And I can hear...

The streets are calling for me. They are calling me to be their advocate—a firm supporter on issues many people overlook or choose to ignore. I speak up for the unheard and defend the defenseless and vulnerable. I choose to be aware of social matters of different ages, sexual orientations, genders, cultures, and races. It makes the soul richer. Most importantly, it makes the world a little bit more civilized, even though it may seem insignificant.

It's in the human nature to be an advocate for something, no matter

what the issue or purpose is.
However, only a few devote their
life, time, and soul to a cause. The
real purpose of social advocating
is not just supporting but believing
in it. True advocacy is not just
what you say or do, but what is
felt when it is said or done. It
is the profound understanding that
every human has the same rights and
needs, no matter what differences
they have. That principle is so
simple, but it is often disregarded.
So often people are treated without
dignity; they are objectified and
misunderstood. These biases are
developed through ignorance, fear,
insecurities, and uncertainties deep
in people's psyches.

    I hope my thoughts and feeling can
inspire a new outlook on society's
troubling mindset. Even if it is
a small transformation, it will
still be noteworthy. People are so
concerned about making a difference
instead of being the difference. I
create some change with my words,
and I am my words. I want to be
that representation for society that
transcends time. I am THE ADVOCATE.

Give Me Liberty . . . Get Rich . . .
Or Give Me Death . . . Die Tryin'

Patrick Henry said, "Give me liberty or
  give me death"
50 Cent said, "Get rich or die tryin"
Sounds like the same shit to me
But now our money became our liberty
It's a reformed term for the modern
  daytime
But I guess when black folks say it
  it's a crime
Honestly I don't see how it's different
And I listen to rap so I'm not going
  to be ignorant
I know rap may seem to glorify violence
But there's a bigger picture. I'm going
  to drop some science
Rap did not create violence; it's in
  our soul
Read the history books, between the
  stories they told
America has always been about "get
  rich or die tryin"
So if they tell you rap is the cause,
  they lyin'.
'Cause if another country makes
  America feel threatened
They got their gang—I mean army—ready
  to cock their weapons
But, for example, if someone
  deliberately threatens my family
And I decide to cock a weapon; I get
  put into the penitentiary
Rehabilitation as they call it, but I
  call it just jail
But by the time we were born, we were
  already locked in a cell
Our minds are confined, and liberty

got us locked up for life without
bail
So how the fuck are we supposed to be
angels if we living in hell
They installed the violent tactics and
tendencies in their own people
And if we show any indication of it, we
are considered evil
America likes identifying its problems
on "us," the target
You want to know why? 'Cause to look
at yourself in the mirror is the
hardest
America got its gangs—I mean army—and
praise them
And when the Bloods and Crips fight,
they just chase them
It's a system I like to call modern-day
slavery
For doing the same shit America calls
bravery
It's just when you are facing racism
and oppression, you attack with
instinct
And violence is what we been taught
since children
Our ancestors forty years ago fought
for their spot and came singing
"Lift every voice and sing"—now we
coming out swinging
So now if the past fighters are dead
or in jail
What you think we going to do now to
excel
We got hip-hop now to represent a
vivid portrayal of our struggle
And America thinks all we doing is
just starting trouble
We're just doing what our forefathers
taught us

But now our lyrics are getting us
    caught up
While Uncle Sam pushes hope not keys
    for our painstaking money

He the real hustler, selling our dream
    for some cream
That's where we learned the game from
They discovered the game way back in
    the day, son
America is the real pimp, hustler, and
    gangster, trust
Yeah, America even pimpin' Mother
    Nature to fuck the weather up
Sticking shit in her butthole to seize
    her energy
Now she got scars and her tears fall
    hard on our country
Don't forget the gold digger Lady
    Liberty, who took our land and lied
to us
So we got to protect our money to gain
    our lack of trust
That goes back to my quotes in the
    beginning
Depicting a continuous quarrel that
    they been winning
Letting us feel guilty for shooting
    someone off-guard
Letting us feel guilty for shooting
    poison in our arms
Letting us feel guilty for selling that
    poison to survive
And feeling guilty for the damaged
    depiction of our daughters and wives
America taught us the game and how to
    live our life
So when we are born with a certain
    skin complexion we have to live in
strife

Black folks been suffering too long
    from betrayals
Plus we got to hear that we are
    nothing from these a-holes
So this struggle been seeping through
    our music

With gospel, blues, jazz, R&B, rock 'n'
    roll, hip-hop, we could live through
it
'Cause culturally we been the most
    influential people of this nation
We got words and a backbone, although
    our bodies are locked in suppression
But check this, we will rise
Trust me, we learned how to strategize
Because America's narrative has been a
    satire
So it's going to be humorous and ironic
    when their scheme backfires
Because spiritually and
    psychologically, black people are
sick
But we sure ain't going die, so America
    better hope we get rich

Broken Windows

Broken windows in broken homes
Heat plaguing the pores of sweated
  domes
The souls of children are hard as
  stone
When Papa creeps and roams from home
His hat is down, making woman moan
As Mama cries buckets of tears for
  foam
To clean her heart away from being
  alone
Who said ya home is ya heart when ya
  heart is torn
The same place where a children's
  future is born
The same place that should be safe but
  they fear it
Poetry is coming out these homes. Can
  you hear it?
The pain is so intense through these
  walls, but can you see it?
Written words left to unlock these
  doors. Can you key in?
It's easy to ignore, because it's
  irrelevant to the world
Don't they know that this is killing
  many boys and girls
It's simple to redirect ya pain on
  someone else
Do you know what happens when you have
  a war rumbling within yourself?
You constantly drain yourself in
  painful memories
You then dig so deep until you lay
  yourself in mental cemeteries
Now you are stuck searching for a lost
  childhood

And this sabotages everything, because
    you are heading in adulthood
So as your life moves forward, you're
    stuck at pause
Searching for tranquility in yourself
    that you lost
And forget about trust, 'cause that's a
    word you will never grasp
People come and go, because you left
    trust in the past
Pain is in your soul, 'cause of mix
    emotions in your head
Your body is in one position as your
    thoughts tread
So many put those thoughts in work and
    in art
Because that's all they can depend on
    in their heart
So broken windows in broken homes will
    never be renovated
And the sweat on sweated domes will
    never be evaporated
Unless they find a form of an
    expression to start over new
Because leftover emotions only turns
    into life's residue
Hopefully families make the right
    decisions for their daughters and
    sons
Because it's better to be from a
    broken home then live in one

Self

My race is black
My ethnicity is Haitian
My ancestry is African
And my citizenship, why, it's American
So I'm struggling with my title
'Cause my people cannot be defined
Our forefathers made sure they
    obliterated our identity
And four hundred years later we are
    debating our name and where we belong
I don't feel American when I walk out my
    house
Whites are American and blacks are called
    "African"-American
Why can't I be just an American? Because
    my skin ain't light enough?
But thinking about it, there is no such
    thing as an American
Like Malcolm said, the only thing
    American about him was his passport
So why should I be called an American if
    America is a false notion
This so-called democracy is executed
    hierarchically, because it's only a few
    people running shit
I mean, the only real Americans are
    the indigenous individuals that were
    slaughtered off
So the "creator" didn't really create
    anything and used my people to build
    this country
They put their blood, sweat, and tears in
    this nation
And they detested every minute of it
So why the fuck should I be called an
    American if I never was one
Since Africans came to Jamestown in 1619,
    they continued to call themselves
    African

By the late 1700s, they were placing
  "African" in front of their churches
But by the late 19th century, they were
  calling us darkies and then Negros.
Later, during Jim Crow, we became colored
And by the 80's we were African-American
And during this period immigrants of the
  same complexions flooded America
But they did not call themselves African,
Rather Haitians, Jamaicans, Trinidadian,
  and so on and so on
So our people were categorizing
  themselves to their countries or
  either our homeland
Which started confusing our people that
  were born here
They weren't born in Africa or the
  Caribbean and couldn't accept the
  American in African-American
And some couldn't trace their ancestry to
  a country in Africa
So what were they? Well, they were just
  black
And, to be honest, I consider myself
  black
Trust, I know in the dictionary they
  define black as wicked
But I was brought up to believe black is
  beautiful
Hey, I'll say it loud, "I'm black and I'm
  proud."
The title "black" offends certain people,
  but that's in my blood.
My music from jazz to rap is black; it's
  in our essence
And on top that, I'm a Haitian woman
I grew up in a separate culture in a
  cubicle called home
My music, food, speech, and traditions
  were diverse
And I'm familiar with the fact Haitians
  are Africans

But I'm proud to be Haitian
I mean, my direct ancestors were slashing
  throats in 1802
They started a revolution that persisted
  for thirteen years
In 1804 we got our independence, and who
  knows where many countries would have
  been
If my people ain't have the balls to
  defeat Napoleon and his pricks
Where would I be?
So I'm proud of my culture, and I can't
  deny my lineage
And it's hard, 'cause I know I'm African
I hear it through our music and taste it
  through our food
Feel it in our rhythm and see it in our
  faces
But it's unfortunate it's not taught in
  our schools
We had the first civilization and
  formulated math, philosophy, and
  hieroglyphics
So what am I, and who I am?
Marcus Garvey was a Jamaican man, but he
  called all of us Africans
And at the same time I'm feeling pompous
  including the Haitian in my name
So where can I find tranquility and
  stability in my identity
Since my struggle and courage is black
And my political ideology is American?
My parents birthed me and made me a
  Haitian
And my blood lingers through some
  country in Africa
Well, I am blACK, I am haitIAN, I am
  "ameriCAN—Fuck that! I'm "United
  StatIAN" and I am afriCAN
And yes, *African* partakes in all the
  above, but my education defines who
  I am

Human
I Am ~~Autistic~~

I was marked on the forehead at
  eighteen months
Stamped with autism
It took a while for me to accept that
  as true
Well, the textbook definition anyway
Because it's obvious
I exhibit a few of the symptoms
For instance
Sometimes I choose not to make eye
  contact
While I listen to the sound of the fan
in the next room
I also might enjoy flapping my arms
Banging my spoon on the table for fun
And, sure, I like pinching arms for
  sensory input
As well as rock back and forth just
  for comfort
I know that's classic autism for you
Don't forget the times I might hit or
  scream
Just to engage in an interaction of
  some kind
The problem with this stamp on my
  forehead
Is that autism is all people see
It's the way people react toward me
Or the reason they simply ignore me
However, I exist beyond the rigid
  diagnosis
The definition
Doesn't tell you that I like hugs and
  tickles
That I like to dance and tap sticks to
  a beat
And that I pick up a computer game

after one try
It does not say I like to chase my
    friends
Or laugh at silly faces
People do not separate me from the
    stamp
I'm one of the same
I'm perceived to be the stamp
And not the stamp being a part of me
So do me a favor
Close your eyes
Just think of one moment in your life
One thing you felt or did, whether
    good or bad
What if you were only known for that
    one thing?
Would that be fair to your character?
No, it would not
People transcend beyond
Any one action
One experience
One thought or feeling in their life
Open your eyes
Now look at me
That is exactly how I feel every day
I'm not just autistic....
I'm a human being

Kids in Hallways

Kids in hallways smoking laced-up weed
Living in nightmares, no traces of dreams
'Cause we were taught it was all about
    the cream
Just get by because the end doesn't
    justify the means
So we murder, steal, and sell drugs to
    survive
Live off food stamps so we can provide
While we live in roach and rat infested
    homes
I swear we can make it out if we invested
    in domes
'Cause our kids rather sell drugs by
    garbage cans
They prefer to look up to the G than a
    garbage man
'Cause a hard-working man can take out a
    wallet and end up dead
Get shot forty times because of a
    situation being misread
Yeah, that's funny; I had to take a laugh
    at that
But all I want to do is spark the
    revolution back
Like Tupac wanted to do before his death
But instead of people doing right they
    rather go left
Nobody wants to hear and see the truth
That's why I use my hands for proof
I write through my vision, mixed with
    complex thoughts
A complex mind developed through
    constant loss
Lost father, lost love, and lost society
    and world
But how can I make a change without
    changing the girl?

So I write about the reality so I can
   overlook the false
Instead of fighting for a boy, I could
   fight for a cause
Instead of riding the rhythm, I make my
   own beats
I just wish that idea could make it out
   to the streets
'Cause kids playing ball to be like
   Michael Jordan
But play the sport without seeing what's
   more important
It's the fundamentals that lead into the
   excellence
But work and passion in the hood lost
   its presence
'Cause now money is everyone's first
   priority
Can you blame us since making it out the
   hood is a hobby?
It's our pastime to struggle out the
   ghettos
Mothers raising kids in this condition
   deserve medals
'Cause black families lose their essence
   daily
After four hundred years, our people is
   still being treated unfairly
It's not racism; it's the society that is
   our Cross
I want us to carry it, but our Christlike
   qualities are lost

Artist

When will real art be respected?
With the absence of gun talk and
  "gangstas gone reckless"
I mean, back in the days N.W.A. was
  the shit
But now it just became plain ridiculous
What happen to the art—hip-hop at its
  best
Now it's more like hip-hop "The
  Business"
To sell some records you have to pop
  a gun
Which shows the lack of quality in
  current albums
Back in the days, you would get to
  know an artist
But now to relate to an artist is the
  hardest
They're so many punch lines that
  albums sound like mixtapes
Someone call 911 'cause hip-hop is
  getting raped
And by the way
Fuck the police, 'cause they wouldn't
  save hip-hop anyway
But it's sad hip-hop is getting fucked
  over
By the people who claim to be hip-hop's
  holder
Who claimed to study the art
And cherish her deep in their hearts
I'm talking about the rappers
Not emcees but rappers
See, through studying hip-hop
I noticed a lot
I noticed that anybody can rap on a
  beat
But anybody cannot be an emcee

I beg to question if anyone cares to
   be one
'Cause it seems like everyone is just
   after the ones
One million, two million, three
   million, four
Thanks, Jay, I see what they aiming for
They aiming for money and fame
And for me to see that, it's a shame
Emcee, please, rappers don't even put
   MC in front of their names
Funny how times have changed
I mean, I would be ashamed if rappers
   now did
Because half of these rappers can't
   obtain what an emcee is
The lack of emceeing is rattling
Shit half these rappers are more prone
   to battling
Back in the days, two artist battling
   was the shit
Lyrics to take out your opponent while
   still having a hit
See, battling was to claim your spot
   in hip-hop
Now it's more like trying not to get
   shot over hip-hop
Let's not even talk about the party
   music
These rappers now are just abusing it
Hip-hop was never a stranger to party
   tracks
But now I'm like "What the fuck is
   that?"
The party anthem is hip-hop's platform
And now it has become a repetitive
   song
That doesn't have as much meaning it
   had back then
I guess I just want the meaning back

again
And hip-hop artist always had a little
  gimmick
But now rappers let the gimmicks
  overshadow the lyrics
That's why there's no stopping this
  growing dynamic
Listeners ride the opinions of people
  on the radio
Without really listening to what's
  coming out their stereo
But I don't want to knock anyone's
  choice in hip-hop
Because whatever you like is going to
  be hot
Hoping it's what you listen to
Instead of what someone told you to or
  not to
Because that's a growing trend
People judging albums without hearing
  a word said
If you didn't "listen" to it, don't
  criticize it
That's just pathetic
Just like the handful of albums I'll
  call classic ten years from now
That's why I respect hip-hop's
  underground
Who never switched their art for money
That's why they get mad love from me
Fortunately, some good-quality artists
  made it mainstream
But still don't get the respect they
  need
I don't want to sound like an anti-new
  school head
'Cause I'm going to love hip-hop
  regardless 'til I'm dead
I'm the biggest hip-hop cheerleader at
  that

I guess I'm just more of an old
    school cat
Everyone wants the money, but what
    happen to the love
Because that's what hip-hop was based
    on from day one
With this topic I can go on forever
But I know for some it's going in one
    ear and out the other
All I want to know is, if someone can
    explain this
What happen to the *art* in *art*ist?

Couple of Seconds

A tattered lip of love
A blackened eye of trust
Is what I see in the bathroom mirror
Behind a locked entrance
Blocking access to robust force
Knowing that at any second
This peace can be knocked down
Or slapped in reckless fear
All I see in this reflection is fright
With a scratched neck of defiance
And a fractured shoulder of control
But behind the discomfort
Is a need for an escape
Because in any second
I will see the black shadow
And the sound of brash footsteps
I look into this mirror
Washing off cherry pain drippings
From cut up forearms of power
And red wrists of restraint
Look at me. I'm scared
Scared to hear him say my name
In that boorish voice that causes
    trembles
All down my back
The same back that I was forced to lie on
But that was not as bad
As bad as my stomach
That was punched and stomped on
My precious lively womb
That became a deadly tomb
In a couple of seconds
So I'm here standing
On black-and-blue thighs of vulgarity
And broken toenails of fight
Because I rather look into this mirror
Than at people
Who look at me in disgust

Whispering in each other's ears
Saying, "Why don't she just leave?"
How weak is she to experience this shame
How can she let him do that to her and
    her baby?
I don't know how
That's why I'm locked in this bathroom
Blocking access to the robust force
Feeling out an escape
Trying to find peace
Even if it is for a couple of seconds
Because every second
Feels like slow-moving eternity
To keeping my sanity
So look at me, mirror
Because I seen this all before
You think this looks bad
You should see my heart

My Cousin Was Blackmailed

Blackmail is the crime of threatening to
   reveal true information about a person
   to the public
Black male is a just a crime, and the
   truth of his history does not want to
   be revealed to the public
Yeah, blackmail, black...mail, black...
   mail—
Get it? A black male
Yeah, 'cause my cousin woke up one day
   and found out he was blackmailed
Not because he was framed or anything,
   just 'cause he was a black male
See the world threatens him through
   oppression, so the truth don't come
   out
They quiet people like Fred Hampton, so
   they won't shout out
The truth—especially when it's coming out
   from a regular black cat
Yeah, a black cat—
The same black-cat superstition that has
   been blamed throughout history for the
   wrongs of the world from the plague to
   blasphemy
But it's funny, 'cause in Japan and
   Britain the black cat is considered
   good luck, but in our dearest USA, its
   bad luck. Isn't that a tragedy?
It's a shame that our own country can't
   give us our forty acres and two mules
   they promised us,
But if we look at the history facts,
   there's not much we can trust
History, hissssstttooorryyyyy, his...
   story
Yeah, *his* fucking *story*

If you don't know who he is or who the
    fuck I'm referring to
Well, I'm talking about people like the
    frontiersmen, pilgrims, KKK, FBI, and
    J. Edgar Hoover too—
Yeah, the founder of the Federal Bureau
    of Investigation
Yeah, an organization that played a part
    in suppressing the black nation
Sort of like the KKK; they were just
    blunter about their hate
But the FBI just would rather set up
    phony investigations, move in, and
    then cover their mistakes
Yeah, that's what happened with the
    assassination of Fred Hampton and the
    Chicago Panther house raid
The truth came out about the FBI's plot,
    but in federal documents the truth is
    vague
Yeah, but "his" truth is vague in the
    minds of real intellects
That won't get trapped in the traps they
    continue to set
'Cause when something goes wrong, it's
    the same ole song—
Yeah, the black song of the black male;
    that's how it is being a black dawg
Yeah, black dawg, black...dawg, black...
    dog—
Get it? Nah, there's no riddle, just
    messing with y'all
But the real black realization has been a
    riddle that can't be solved
So how are we going to get education and
    stay out of prison if we can't evolve
Yeah, they treat us like animals, but
    y'all haven't seen the real animal in
    us yet

When the time comes, we will be ready—
    don't fret
See, I was reading a piece on J. Edgar
    Hoover, and I found out he had
    connections with the Mafia, so he could
    obtain info to blackmail
I just find it funny, 'cause he was the
    direct connection to frame the black
    male—
Extrajudicial punishment, as they call it
    to be
But I call it punishment by complexion
    that some are deemed
To have through the miracle of their
    birth
'Cause having the complexion of mine is
    just a curse
And I'm not trying to denigrate the name
    of white people
'Cause even Malcolm at one point had to
    admit they all weren't evil
I just don't want black people to feel
    it's okay to just settle
And I'm just trying to take that idea and
    push it to the next level
By putting the truth out in my poetry
    and changing the minds that been
    blinded by this false illusion
'Cause, like Fred Hampton said, you can
    kill the revolutionary, but you can't
    kill the revolution

Last Night

He seduced me with his eyes
Touch me thoroughly through the inside
He made me feel comfort
Answered my thoughts like an expert
It was instant lust at first, I'll admit
Because his potential and confidence were
   legit
But deep admiration followed suit
After witnessing what his hands can do
His personality—resilient but still
   sensitive
Made all my problems feel relevant
And he said he could take them away in a
   heartbeat
And when he said that, he meant it
   literally
Every breathtaking beat
I felt the pressure rising from my feet
It was intense meetings and long nights
Every word he spoke was so right
But Dad hated his guts and shook his
   head
At the sight of him, my mom's face
   turned red
They just knew he was here to take their
   only baby
Friends agreed, saying that I was crazy
And maybe I was—I been depressed for
   years
He knew exactly how to address my fears
He said he'd leave if I stayed with
   friends and family
So I pleaded, *"Please* don't leave me
They are my past and you're my future
   indeed
Just love me forever pretty pretty
   please."
I ran after him, trying to keep pace

I pulled his black hood off, covering his
   face
He turned around, looking at my drizzling
   eyes
He realized I meant what I said for the
   first time
He extended his hand and said, "Come
   with me
Together we will be for eternity
I nodded my head yes and left a note on
   my nightstand
Together we walked as he held my right
   hand
My mom found my note the next day
Her mouth opened with no words to say...

Last night I committed suicide
Don't ask why
I'm not still alive
To say these words
But if you haven't heard
Last night I committed suicide

ABCs, Part 1

I'm an advocate against adolescents
   afflicting adversity
Because brothers boasting 'bout bullshit
   and blasphemy
Causes a corrupted country considering
   conflicting causalities
Derived deep down from devious
   debaucheries
Effecting our existence estimating from
   empty elements of education
Furthermore, against forenamed frauds
   called fathers who flee from the family
   foundation
Generating gangstas gunning and getting
   grimy against the government
By heavily hauling hundreds of homies
   into halfway houses because of hasty
   harassment
These idiots instigated ignorance against
   infants and made intellectuals feel
   inarticulate, making their IQ and
   identities an illusion
Since integration, they inflicted
   their ill-advised ideologies on the
   indigenous and black individuals'
   institutions
Justice is just a justification for jail
   to jeopardize our Jedi mind journeys
Jerks jacked up our judgment to join
   the average Joes, jades, juveniles,
   jailbirds, and junkies
Killing negativity and curiosity will be
   the key to kick-starting knowledge of
   our kids
And karma is coming for kidnapping our
   culture and the killing of our kin

I Wish You Murdered Her

She lies lifeless in her bed
As the light bulb flashes from dark to
  light
The shaky ceiling fan creaks
Her body is naked, cold, and covered with
  fright

I wish you murdered her!
Because death was merely the next step
Murder might have been easier
As she replays how everything went
Constant flashes of shame in sight
An Atlantic ocean of tears
Her trust collapsed in seconds
Though it was built and matured through
  years
She sees your reflection in the corner of
  her eye
And still doesn't know her vision is
  distorted
Now your eyes are imprinted in her brain
As the idea of safety is aborted

I wish you murdered her!
Because all she hears is time passing
Ticks and tocks of terror
How will she get out of her bed
When black clouds follow her like the
  weather
She can feel your skin on top of her
The sweat under her fingertips
Your hot breath on her neck
But worse, the stamped fingers in a fist

I wished you murdered her!
Because a glass of water will never taste
  the same

Glass shattered in little fragments like
    her heart
When you broke in and busted the door
    chain
The scent of mandarin berry candles
Is now the scent of death
She lost the sense of herself
Everything that felt right in her life is
    now left
I wished you murdered her!
Because when police came knocking on her
    door
She ignored the service and blocked her
    ears
As her eyes fixated on the evidence of
    rape on the floor

Black as a Purse

I was ashamed because they said my skin
    was black as a purse
And to have a name like mine is only a
    curse
They said in the black of my house, I was
    doing voodoo
And that my father's father was called
    Shaka Zulu
That was supposed to be an insult by the
    way
And I took it as one, wishing I wasn't
    black today
Wish I wasn't a criminal, 'cause crime
    don't pay
Fuck that, it has to, 'cause them racist
    folks set the stage
And, look, them motherfuckers built the
    murder capital of the world
And I'm supposed to be this innocent
    black college girl
Fuck that; yeah, fuck that. My mind's too
    different to be like everyone else
Ignoring people as they wonder why I
    stick to myself
'Cause I have to, since my mind is an
    institution
That is mentally fighting a televised
    revolution
But only I can see the damage, war, and
    the pain
Holding tissues to wipe the blood licking
    out my brain
It's a fucking shame—and not my
    complexion by the way
Because the best things come in different
    forms and shades
And I'm supposed to appreciate it and
    celebrate one month out the year

Yeah, I'm *black*, but I'm supposed to put
   my head back down when March appears
Damn, we're even told when to celebrate
   our blackness
We should know good ideas aren't so good
   in practice
'Cause during black history month, I
   didn't learned a damn thing
And these kids today only know Martin
   Luther King
And not the real one—no, the
   commercialized Dr. King
One day, one speech, one line, "I have a
   dream" Dr. King
He had a dream, and we broadcast it, but
   can't bring it to reality
And I'm crying tears of ink, because I'm
   starting to believe it's a fantasy
I have a dream, but I'm fighting for it
   to be heard
And I'm not fighting people—but my own
   words
My own soul is dying, and my voice is
   falling off like a petal
But I'm that concrete rose, intellectual
   chick rising out the ghetto
And I refuse to let anyone take that
   away from me
Especially not a dick that's in a young-
   minded boy's jeans
Especially not a dick that believes
   there's no nightmare in our American
   dream
'Cause I'm too smart and real to fall for
   that—I got the power
I might have a soft voice, but I ain't a
   fucking coward
I'm not afraid to say we are hypocrites
   when there is genocide in Danfur

We are *killing* Iraqis every day, and we
    don't know what for
I'm ashamed not because of my complexion
But for my generation
And for the next that's coming up
'Cause we pushing keys, basketballs, and
    raps songs, before knowledge, which is
    a must
And I'm not hating on Black History
    Month, 'cause yours truly was born on
    the fourteenth
But black history being history every
    day of the year is my dream

Built to Destroy

I was built to destroy lives
Break down minds
Faith depletes behind my trouble lines
I'm a graphic energy in disguise
A misguided sign
But still I'm a symbol of mankind

I was built to destroy lives
I am the misery in mother's cries
My poison pierces through your insides
To prove that numbers don't lie
Thirty thousand fall to my fatal
    seduction annually
Because my owners give me strength
    manually
I get high; I load up on powder
Spit lead to crease power
I give weak minds force through their
    fingertips
No one is safe, not even the innocent
So I have numerous bodies under my
    muzzle
And it's the families that I leave
    distraught and puzzled
Left to fix the pieces from my dominance
I always feel at home; I live in domestic
    violence
I constantly have women on their backs
But that's not all, I'm the leading cause
    of death for young blacks
And apparently the police are the last to
    react
Which makes my job a little easier to
    execute
Somehow my mission is strong against
    blacks and the destitute
Death and critical condition is my
    everyday language

But I'm a saving grace for the owners
   that can't manage
I am the end of suicidal thoughts
A helping trigger hand for a life lost
I aided so many, but murder was the case
   that they gave me
But inside I wish someone could save me
Because I just wanted to serve and
   protect somebody
Use me to hunt so men can provide for
   their families
But now I'm just casting tears on lone
   lovers
Because now men use me to hunt each
   other

I was built to destroy lives.
I might have claim a few daughters, a few
   wives
Some fathers, some smokers, some sun
   tanners
As time goes on I increase my standards
But as you can see I'm not prejudice
With my ego, I might just be a tad bit
   rebellious
I just get upset when so-called
   specialist, call me malignant
How is that supposed to make me
   feel during my awkward stages of
   development?
So I might run away and spread through
   the bloodstream
Or the lymph node system to blow off
   steam
I know the chances of us bumping heads
   gets stronger with time
But I'm known to have encounters with
   children at their prime.
I give them a fight, pull out their hair

But for what it's worth, I know it's
  unfair
Whether I am a damaged gene or inherited
You decide to kill all cells just so I
  will be irrelevant
Put your body and soul on the line to
  depart from knowing me
To only progress and radiate through
  therapy
Whether its tears or body, I use up your
  tissues
But I'm also dealing with conflicting
  issues
I'm social; I love people, every part,
  every cell.
But you will know my presence with every
  lump, every swell
And when people survive my combative
  stage it changes life for good.
My demeanor is obnoxious, but I'm really
  misunderstood
For everyone that endures my tough
  times, I try to cease
And because of my temper, so many are
  left decease
Cause when I get mad I spread with
  uncontrollable fury
While millions of people walk just to
  cure me
I know the world wants me to be benign
But what they don't realize is, so do I

I was built to destroy lives
My seismic activity builds up in size
My energetic waves swim in the earth's
  crust
I hold back remembering the
  infrastructures I've crushed
I like to keep things in but cave under
  pressure

Eventually leading to enormous shaking
    and ground rupture
Causing many to be compressed in gravel
And destruction and pain are the
    elements unravel
Families destroyed and areas left in
    shard
The blatant images of devastation makes
    my job hard
Especially if my outburst is at magnitude
    seven
The only solace I have is hoping there's
    a heaven
With the serious damage it's good to have
    hope on the flip side
Because I need some peace on the inside
Since I have to experience people lying
    under rocks
I'm the one left astonished in a state of
    aftershock
Pondering why I must come with such cost
A whole country grieving for their own
    loss
Children becoming orphans in a matter of
    seconds
It's difficult to look at my nature as a
    blessing
And the more shallow I am the more
    dramatic
Which means the stress of the humans
    becomes more traumatic
I displace homes, roads, the entire
    appearance
While I become a country's ultimate human
    experience
Moving desolation through my seismic
    waves
Striking physical darkness living in mass
    graves

My discomfort hits higher off the Richter
   scale
Because these people are witnesses and
   living it as well
I'm causing these people an out-of-body
   encounter
Where their senses shifts in space and
   matter
But it was the flood of people that came
   to the rescue,
Revealing people can exist in pain, which
   I can attest to
It gives me some solace knowing the human
   race can be selfless creatures
And the helpful spirits cause them to
   become each other's healers
And that chemistry plays a part in my
   significance
That's all I can say when the world
   questions my existence
See, I wish my geological faults didn't
   have to kill man
But somehow that's all a part of God's
   plan

The Thinker

Now I was hydrated, rested, and ready to reach back to the Elders with these amazing finds. The air was cool, and the land was alluring as it shined off the sun's light. I continued to walk peacefully in this remote territory.

Instantly I was hit with a sudden vision. It was a vision of a place that was familiar and unfamiliar at the same time. I analyzed every detail and felt every emotion. I felt at ease with the big, brown, rusted, old buildings. The one that seemed most clear was labeled "2 4 8." The vision was a comfortable connection with my thoughts and my eyes. I continued to discover . . .

I explore the world through my mind. I live through life with thoughts shifting with time and energy. Thoughts are behind our actions, emotions, memories, and beliefs, and without the thoughts, humans would not exist. The mind is the driving force of our beings. Thinking keeps us healthy and gives us the ingredients for survival. We process thoughts to advance every second. That is why the brain is the most interesting and complex organ. It was created to be an infinite creator.

It is up to the world's creatures to shape their own purpose and the world's revolution through the brain. It is the most distinctive feature that moves in this universe. The mind gives individuals their own logic as to whom and why they are in existence. Although everyone has a mind, everyone will not discern their potential life discovery. In reality, people utilize a small percentage of their mind, which displays how powerful the use of the brain is when exercised.

The best thing about the mind is that it is endless. We think the minute we are born, and we die with a final thought. Every life moment or movement has a thought associated with its presence. Most significantly, thought lasts forever, even when the physical is gone. With the function of thought, people can still be alive after death, because of other people's reflections.

So these words I write have a deeper meaning for me. These ideas I cultivate live their own life. I give birth to them, but their value lies not only with me but with others who experience them. My thoughts made me who I am, and I use it as my faith. It is my spirituality, my emotions, and my mentality. However, my thought is not me—it is beyond me. The quantity and quality of my life is yet to be determined, but my thoughts will always be here today and forever. I am THE THINKER.

February 14, 1986

The day that Mother Nature sneezed throughout the earth's smoke and Mother Love gave out her overused candy and chocolate to her children.

I came,

Fighting through the walls of my mother, gasping for air three months early. Everyone was watching me like a horror movie, but I was just a one-pound treat before the previews.

Those silly people told my mother I was with Mr. Death. But I was just on a date! They should have known I was going to come back. This is cliché, but he took my breath away—too fast! He was introducing me to his family in the heavens our first date. Man, I'd been waiting six months to get home; I just wanted to go back.

And the next thing I knew I was in my Father's arms. He was telling me I was special and that I was a love baby. I came out before the month of flowers in search of Mr. Right, and at that moment I thought I found him, until . . .

Mr. Right became Mr. Rolling Stone, leaving his hat on different beds and the rims of 70 proof bottles. He never left his hat with me, just his image. And because of that I cursed myself out in the mirror.

At 9, I meant Mr. Drug Dealer. He used to wait for me on the corner of my block with a used cereal box of white cornflakes; I used to watch him give it out to everyone in the neighborhoods. He was a plague to everyone he knew. He robbed me every day for my ice cream money until the ice cream truck stop coming.

Then at 10, I found Mr. Radio. I stayed up all night with him under my covers, trying to find out all his secrets and his special language. We were inseparable until . . .

I found Mr. Bed-Stuy and Mr. Flatbush. They taught me how to maneuver in the streets, how to look out for myself, and who to trust. They taught me to keep my friends close and enemies closer. And they lead me right into . . .

Mr. Rape. He caught me by surprise. I lost many things from him like trust, sleep, and my virginity. But I gained some things too, like longer showers, silent days, and my Chap Stick on the rims of 70 proof bottles.

Then I meant Mr. Poetry at 12. He showed me how to express my feeling without telling anyone. My secrets and ideas stayed between us. He stayed by my side, even when I ignored him for . . .

Mr. Dance. But four years later, Mr. Dance left me by hitting a bat on my knees. Luckily, I had Mr. BK and Mr. LF as good friends. They helped me pick up the pieces and focus on school. They even went with me on the bus rides to see Mr. Rikers for four years.

At 18, I met Mr. Temple. Our connection came naturally. He introduced me to different kinds of people. He gave me a voice to speak my opinion and even brought me back to Mr. Poetry.

At 21, I met Mr. Philly. He showed me a different perspective on trust. On the outside he is real gritty, but sometimes I see the signs of brotherly love.

Now at 22, I'm about to meet Mr. Graduation. He wrote me a letter telling me to meet him in May. I'm anticipating what he is waiting to tell me. Hopefully he can help in my search for Mr. Right.

Genius Period

Racked up with all this information
Thoughts moving slowly information
My heart might come complacent
But my mind capitalizes on creation
See, my mental frame is enlighten
Where logic becomes exciting
Theory becomes insight
Ideas are forethought but eyes . . . foresight
So, basically I'm borderline smart and crazy
Normal minds go straight; mine is sorta mazy
Being genius is hazy
But it's what you do with it that's extraordinary
I guess that's how Cobain felt in the attic
The pressure caused him to used deadly tactics
I wish it was simple mathematics
Staying cool, trying your
hardest to be diplomatic
But the only outcomes are the
behaviors of an addict
Your mind can be a gift and also your bad habit
Many people have these great abilities
I just don't want to be the one
to lose that tranquility
My forte could go past normal capacity
But I must stay grounded . . . gravity
It's not physics, but Sir Newton
was past greatness
And it was after his death when
he really got his praises
I just want to prove to myself that I can make it
Real courage passes all the ignorant fake shit
I don't want to come off ill-mannered
I just place myself at a higher standard
I want to be that power that
flows through the wire
Have a strong sense of strength
and walk through the fire

So when thoughts go roaring, I'm
not looking for a cop-out
Instead Ima use it as success, no drop out
Just be a product of my mentality
Cuz if this psych degree won't,
this psyche will carry me
My words and this progressing flow
With thoughts no man should ever go
See, growing up I thought there
was something wrong with me
But this might set me apart from
the rest of humanity
I'm not saying I'm a genius—
just want a genius period
Just want to be the best at what I do—Period

Untitled

Want to know why
My flow delivers like Chinese food
And words teach knowledge, minus school
'Cause I live for hours in this reflective no man's
    land—
And poof! I write out who I lyrical am
Because I am the bottom thought you have when
    you're high
And I am that truth squared in your circle of
    lies
Because I rise above any pigeonhole you try to fit
    me in
And at my demise, my ridged soul won't be filled
    with sin
It will be filled with misunderstood verses and
    misquoted lines
It's almost intellectual ignorance to ignore this
    misfit's mind
I'm a rebel of the heart and the genius of the
    eyes
And my verbal style is free the way I improvise
Misread rhymes nurse the drive to write to keep
    the sanity
I hold back, knowing that many won't understand me
So I write going right, knowing there are no
    rights to gravity
Tomorrow this life can be gone, and my one
    accomplishment would be this poetry
For a while I was ashamed to claim that as true
Hoping I have more to offer the world, and maybe
    I do
But writing is the one thing I have great
    expectations that I live up to
And poetry hurts my soul when it's absent in my
    life the way love do
So I nurture this craft, because it is my first-
    born skill

I birth this talent and won't be taken away
    against my strength and will
So I adopted this pen and pencil, hoping I don't
    lose this gift
These aspirations are real, but any self-doubt
    can make this a myth
My flow can start delivering like digiorno pizza,
    and my words can become jokes
I learned to glue the thoughts to the page and
    let it elevate above the strokes
So I keep these words flowing and lines constantly
    written
Because this is more than an art as a pastime—
    this is my life exhibition

Garbage

I live in the middle of the hood
Where I get off subways and get beamed with
   helicopters lights
The type of hood where there are beer delis in
   the center of every block
And where gunshots pop like microwave popcorn

I work at the beginning of suburbia
Where I walk off the bus and people think I'm
   homeless
The place where Starbucks are the new corner
   stores
And a Honda has the same value as a scooter

Being in the presence of both
I came to a marvelous conclusion
Garbage is garbage in the hood and in suburbia
It still smells the same . . . like shit
Except in the hood we put out our garbage every
   day, anytime, and don't care who's watching
Whereas in suburbia they have regulations on
   their trash
When to put it out, how big it has to be, how to
   do it on holidays
And you can't forget to break the cardboard boxes

I know you thinking garbage is petty
How can I compare neighborhoods by their trash?
I should be looking at the salaries and MDs and
   PhDs—
Well, *please*.
All right, I know the money and the status means
   something in America
But it means nothing if your trash is so bad that
   you can get out of it
How bad your shit is plays a major role in how
   good your shit can be

I'm not making excuses, but it's the truth
But just because it's the truth is not a
    justification to let other motherfuckers' trash
    be better than yours
Especially if you work harder and have a stronger
    nose to deal with shitty garbage
See, when people from the hood make it to the
    top, it is more rewarding, because it's harder
    to accomplish through all the shitty, smelly
    trash
Than having how-to guidelines for every house on
    every block
In the just-as-shitty suburbia
And when I live in suburbia—because I'm going to
    play the American game too
I'm not going to shit on the neighborhood,
    because it is not their problem I grew up in a
    big pile of garbage
But I am going to shit on those how-to
    guidelines, because I know how to keep my shit
    clean
But don't worry; I came from the hood with a
    degree
So I'll still keep it classy with a scent of
    perfume

Blue I and II

If poetry was Harlem, I'd be Langston Hughes
Or I would be Lady Holiday, but I write my own
    blues
Blue like the colorful words I use
Matter of fact, my colorful words have their own
    hue
Because my words get their pigment through my
    visual cues
Then magically travels to the page and sticks
    like glue

My poetry is as blue as the tears my pen cries
As it weeps through the loose-leafs on blue lines
See, I'm blue like Miles and as jazzy as bebop
Classic . . . but still fresh like my name was
    hip-hop
My voice is calm and scenic like the blue ocean
But can cause ripple effects through this verbal
    motion
And I might just lure you in with this blue-and-
    black potion
'Cause my poetry is not just words but an art
    explosion

Fashion Sense

My self will outlast my being
Because my body is just a daily outfit
That I wear for the world
It's a fashion symbol of being human
I sport the "girl" day and evening attire—
You know, a beautiful vagina with matching
     breasts.
But, honestly, I wear it to fit in
With the rest of the moving corpses that are
     rocking
"The human look"
I believe to make it, assimilation has to be
     tried on
So I go into the fitting room with the same vagina
     and breasts
But I always felt that look was played out
Out of style with no fashion sense
Because luckily I have some common sense
My brain, my heart, and my soul are more my style

My *brain* is the purse I could wear every day
Thoughts,
Ideas,
Dreams,
Beliefs,
Opinions.
It never goes out of style, because I can wear it
     with any outfit.
I can wear it with a sweat suit
Or with couture.
Although purses vary and might get overloaded at
     times,
They always make the outfit complete

My *heart* is the jewelry I will always have
But don't always choose to wear

I can put
    it
    on
        or
            take
                it
                    off
But when I choose to put it on, my feelings shine
                    I have a glow everyone sees
It is mostly real, but it is often imitated
However, I have some fake ones for the haters

Then there is my *soul*, which is like the perfect
    and classic *black shoe*
I have a personality that goes with any fashion

High fashion
With the rich, stuck-up, "I have money you will
    never have," moving corpses

Catalog fashion
With the middle-class, "I'm going to Starbucks on
    my lunch break" corpses
                    Or the going-out-with-the-
    girls "because it's ladies' night" attire
                    Over the "I have a man I go
    home to" outfit that only he sees

The punk/ gothic
With the "I don't give a fuck; I am who I am. You
    can suck my dick" wear

Or street wear
With the hood rich people who wear clothes worth
    more than their salary with the occasionally
    "my mommy bought it for me" look

See, the image of me that people see doesn't
    have the affect my thoughts, feelings, and
    personality will have on the world

I'm not going to lie; sometimes I get sucked in
   by the other corpses
And think this body means something valuable
So I shop till I drop for some confidence, because
   their image left an impression on me
But that second impression does not stand close
   to years of impressions in the future
After my outfit is buried, because there is no
   more tailoring to be done
My purse, jewelry, and classic black shoes will
   live on
So, what's your style?

Deep Wounds

I got deep wounds the surgeon can't cut
Physical pain a hit man can't touch
Felt the throbbing in the pit of my gut
Losing you was nothing like losing trust
See, I hid behind you and your tough insight
That is exactly why I used to cover you in light
Didn't want anyone else to know the truth
'Cause I would have to speak of what you do
So I kept the back of my tunnel dark
Without you I didn't see the trouble I was 'bout
     to embark
Life got cold alone in a room with windows open
Vulnerable and empty—no time for moping
Around in a town just as rotten as the apple
Looking at a rusty old pen like a scalpel
Since you backstabbed me and left like my dad did
You just vanished, and I'm trying not to keep you
     as baggage
'Cause I see traces of you in my beat-up notebooks
It's amazing how you stole my image like a photo
     crook
Regardless, I decided to live life without you
     beside me
The pain is always inevitable, but luckily love
     was timely
So it was hard not to be able to talk about the
     newfound passion
The exhilaration and bliss I was trapped in
So I took classes on you to get you back in my
     hands
But it was too technical, and my love was not
     advanced
So I got a B, just a B—wasn't good enough for an
     A
And I wanted to blame the teacher and say he was
     an A
Hole, but he couldn't fix the hole in my heart

If I was not the needy mechanic trying to fix the
    parts
So literally I deserved an F for forgetter
And now I know you are saying, "Fuck, I wish I
    never met her"
Because I forgot about the other things you used
    to do.
And now all my friends ask about you
Why I didn't fight and how they miss hearing your
    voice
And thinking about it now I had a choice
But I chose to give up on you and our chemistry
Science wasn't the funniest subject, but English
    was just right for me
I miss talking through your syllables; the lines
    were so potent
And you stuck with me no matter how many days I
    went
Without writing to you, leaving you half alive,
    breathing for a word
So to keep lashing out when I should embrace you
    is absurd
You came back to me when in reality you shouldn't
Because it was me who left you, when I knew I
    couldn't
Work out the drama, the love, the intricate
    language
That was almost ten years ago today; I just
    couldn't seem to manage
See, I left you because I was afraid
Everyone would ask to hear what you tell me every
    day,
Ask me to repeat your advice and publish it to
    the world
I was afraid of the image of you that was just a
    quiet girl
That had strong volume through a script that
    wasn't oral
And now for the first time, the mouth and hands on
    in quarrel

Because now that you are back, I want something
    in addition to the lines
I want a voice that goes with the verbal rhymes
I might be asking for a lot, since I left you,
    but I just don't want to depart
So, Poetry, can you forgive me and once again
    become my art

Going Back to Brooklyn

As I leave Philly for the hundredth time
I prepare myself for the adventure I used to call
my life, Brooklyn
Hoping I'm not leaving one miserable place to go
back to another
So when I reach the Empire State
I step into the soil of Manhattan that is not so
Harlem
See, I was raise in NY, but Manhattan was a
getaway for me
It was a place to breathe and relax while a
million people bump into me
Because in that borough people walked on running
feet
So as I stood on Manhattan's not-so-Harlem soil
I crossed my fingers hoping that Brooklyn was
different now, a place to breathe
So I rode the A train to respond to this
aspiration
The A train is a magical capsule that takes me
from Manhattan to Brooklyn
In a total of five minutes
As I sit in the rectangle contraption
I pray that my birthplace looks and smells
different
Hoping there are no more pharmacists selling
pain-starters on the corners
No more salespeople selling everything but
freedom on Utica
No more preachers rapping their homemade Jay-z
lyrics in front of their stoops
No more supermodels walking down Flatbush in not-
so-real but affordable Gucci heels
And as I hit the red, white, and black Fulton and
Utica stop
I see something across the platform that tells me
things are the same
I see a gentleman in a red and black, fitted,

111

Red button-down with black buttons with a white
  tee under it
Black jeans with red stitching,
Red and black sneaks—and can't forget the white
  doo rag hanging out his pocket
It is like he purposely wanted to match the
  subway platform
Being raise in Brooklyn, that wouldn't be a
  surprise
So I reluctantly went up the subway stairs to see
  Brooklyn again
It was the same shit, but deep in my heart I
  kinda liked it
I ran to catch the blue-and-white, two-dollar
  vehicle
So I could stop at memory lane right on Lenox
  Ave.
As soon as I reached it, it was clear Brooklyn
  and I were the same
I ran into the corner store with fifty cent to buy
  colored sugar
Walked up my block, and ignored the guy and the
  rest of his dawgs
Who were pissing at me like I was a cat
Hey, I might have a pussy, but I'm no fucking
  animal
I ran up the half-wood /half-nothing/ half-
  landlord, don't-do-shit stairs
And opened the door to the aroma of roach spray
  and groit with piklis on top
I gave all the forty people in my house kisses on
  the cheek
Sat on the bed, kicked off my shoes, and put my
  feet on the floor
Hoping I didn't step on a mouse trap
And as sweat trickled down my forehead
I sat in front of the fan, singing "Candy Rain"
  like I did fifteen years ago
I pulled out my Sour Power and thought life
  couldn't get better than this

This is when I realized I could always breathe in
    Brooklyn
But I needed to breathe on my own
In another miserable place, to make it
    unmiserable
Because even though I'm in the best place in the
    world, I still long for Philly
My home—another miserable but not so miserable
    place

Mind and Love

Mind over matter
The weak always choose the latter
Ideas build substance steadily
And gradually objects lose intensity
To know that Logic is a lethal method
A casual weapon
Enforced in the mind when rightly done
Develops strength and births wisdom
'Cause Knowledge means shit without being wise
See, matter changes, but the mind has to be
    exercised
Acquiring space and time embodies the world's
    existence
But the mind makes everything else work in an
    instant
See, Matter represents the civilians, but mind is
    the master
And with your third eye you can see past the
    matter faster

Love over war
Which is really worth fighting for?
Both are necessary for survival
War is an art against its revival
But love is a battlefield full of hurt
Using a shield of trust to protect its turf
It strengthens the soul and fights against pain
In war, the best armor is to just stay out of
    range
Victory isn't guaranteed in love or war
But Love rules its kingdom without a sword
War is more than just people that die in combat
Love hurts, but with death there is no coming
    back
War is a virtue of courage but also represents
    sin
Because it takes years of love to make a man and
    seconds of war to destroy him

Memory's Secret

Vision is my memory's secret
And my ears have my mouth speechless
Not 'cause I can't talk; I just don't say bullshit
Less you talk, the more your words sounds like
   good shit
I let me words stand out alone; don't need
   persuasion
As my vision and my words flows through
   integration
My ears got my mouth pacing, tracing for words to
   draw
But my vision don't need protection 'cause,
   oooowww, baby, I like it raw
Through experience I learned to look at the world
   inside and out
Inside my heart and bullshit out other people's
   mouths
'Cause that's where you see the worst in human
   nature
And I learn that whatever I believe is major
I don't discount the no's, and sometimes yeses
   are cheap blows
They dig holes in the unbelievable
And no's never get to the unreachable
So I say the fuck-yous, but I say it out of love
'Cause I love myself too much for a cheap shove
Don't ever try to screw me over with words, 'cause
   I taste and hear shit
My ears, mouth, and eyes is an impervious
   tri-unit
I combine them into one like the Holy Spirit
So for the faithful, through my words their soul
   I merit
My complex brain goes through compulsion when
   they combine
Shit I knew when I was born that I was divine
I'm God's gift, 'cause he gave me breath when I
   wasn't breathing

And he gave me my voice when I never started
    screaming
So the miracle day of my birth with the day of my
    struggle
Gave me a fateful complex added to a heart that
    is humble

Ghetto Spaceship

*These are the days life is better lived through
escaping*
*When you feel like your dreams aren't worth
chasing*
These are the days when you just can't face shit
*Hoping you could just ride out in the ghetto
spaceship*

See, I know the feeling of living life from bad
news to bad news
Phone calls from bill collectors instead of calls
for interviews
Work days get longer while my paycheck gets
smaller
And even putting a smile on my face gets a little
harder
Never thought getting my hair washed would become
a luxury
Or going over budget meant ordering a five-dollar
meal at Wendy's
Overdraft and negative balance becomes everyday
language
And I can't bear the thought of people thinking
that I can't manage
Asking for help sounds like you're a bum asking
for a handout
Instead of jiggling a cup, I'm praying that any
minute something will pan out
And the lack of money transfers transfers to my ego
It's missing in action like Shaq throwing a free
throw
I tell myself it will get better in the future,
to give me some relief
But it doesn't really work if the thought is not a
belief
So it feels good once in a while, when I can get
a laugh in

But I still walk around knowing any minute
    something can happen
So I constantly walk with that bad feeling in my
    chest
Waiting for my ghetto spaceship. . . . Shit, my
    mom got cancer in her breast

These are the days you could have more patience
Convincing yourself that you're the therapist, but
    you're really the patient
These are the days you give out advice you can't
    give yourself—that's bullshit
Flying away, facing the truth is harder on the
    ghetto spaceship

Still haven't faced the truth, so I can't be the
    best caregiver to my mom
People think I'm handling it so well, but it's
    really me being withdrawn
I know blood is thicker, but sometimes I feel
    like water.
Dealing with the fact I never been the best
    daughter
I can barely say I love you when in my heart I
    really do
So I make sure I go to the appointments and talk
    to the doctors as a substitute
I can't tell her she is strong, but I can ask if
    she took her medicine
So much fear, but holding on to the fact cancer
    is a battle she can win
I can't save her, but I know in my heart she can
    handle anything
I wish I had superman powers, 'cause I would save
    her and him—
My boyfriend—but I would be kryptonite if he knew
    I tried to
He turns down my help, but I can't complain,
    'cause I do it too

We both don't want to be a burden to the other,
    but it causes us pain
So we're holding each other up but still standing
    in the rain
We give each other so much joy than anyone would
    every know
But we have to hold in the back of our minds we
    might have to let each other go
We refuse to make that hard decision, so we fight
    each day, hoping things change some
I'm not Sam, but in my heart I believe it's slow
    but a change gonna come
In time we both know if things don't shape up
Our worse fear will rise in our ghetto spaceship,
    and we will have to break up

These are the days you lie around wasting
Not really satisfied, but you become complacent
These are the days you try to convince yourself
    life is a gift
But you're feeling cursed, so you ride out in your
    ghetto spaceship

I tell myself I'll live through it, because I have
    to, to tell the truth
When my boost of confidence just passes through
    like the juice
In my mind, all the negative thoughts hold on so
    strong
And I can't tell people everything that's really
    going wrong
So I say I'm okay, but I'm really thinking the
    opposite
When what's really on my mind is just politics
Like Maher and Clinton—you know, just Bills
And of course the other drama causing these
    mental ills
The only solution my family can say is to go back
    to college
But my problem is me, not acquiring the knowledge

Matter of fact, college has been a pain in the ass
Because now I'm paying an arm and a leg for that
    pointless class
And I blame college for making me feel so
    entitled
To a great job the economy apparently can't
    handle
And thinking of owning the government more money
    scares me
As long as I get a job that will pay for me
But in reality I don't even know what I want to do
'Cause everything I did was to please my family,
    and now I'm confused
So going back to school this time is an option
    not an obligation
Until I can figure out *my* path with this
    miseducation
Like I said before, the problem has always been me
My lack of confidence and fight has enabled me not
    to succeed
And realizing I can't save everyone only myself
And knowing it's okay sometimes to ask for the
    help
And telling someone something at some point might
    lead to internal bliss
All those sayings I say can become beliefs not
    myths
But Ima ride out with the spinning rims and the
    hydraulics on my fantasy whip
Hoping writing this all for the first time can be
    my ghetto spaceship.

Most Wanted

I want to be inspired.

That union of the five senses
Motivated to open the mind's defenses
Between that infatuation of life and art
Leading to a mental project provoked by the heart

I want to be imagined.

That picture of thought
Where ideas are trained after they're caught
That concept tangled in the mind's eye
Erupting the passion of being inscribed

I want to be written.

That stroke of printed genius
Where the mind is an expressive strategist
And the hand is a pawn under the heart's
    supervision
To compose a colorful black-and-white
    transcription

I want to be read.

Caught in translation
A terminology that leads to its own
    interpretation
A subjective masterpiece before it is assessed
To induce naturally an objective analysis

I want to be memorized.

That committed recollection
Exercising brainpower with an intention
To let the memory's keeper play its part
Because learning something has to be known by
    heart

I want to be heard.

That perception of sound
Where the tone makes the expression profound
The ear is an instrument to navigate a cerebral
    link
With a vivid voice compelling the soul to think

I want to be loved.

That ultimate symbol of reverence
Where time is not time but an experience
Trust has no boundaries and gets stronger with
    its absence
And the meaning at the core validates deep
    substance

I want to be that poem.

American Made

As a kid I thought I would make *it* without a
   problem
Learned the hard way that my race and gender were
   a problem
Trust me, the last thing I'm doing is making
   excuses
Just telling you what the truth is
I thought if I graduated college, I would make it
   in America
But somehow I lost myself and became damn afraid
   of her
Like she was too good for me, too rich, and
   beautiful for me
So somehow I believed I was poor and ugly
Therefore I became my biggest enemy
My mentality and ability parted their chemistry
And literally I became a nonentity, because I
   felt defeated
And my purpose in this world was depleted
Which meant the system was working appropriately
Because apparently
The Oprahs make it through coincidentally
Or should I say "affirmatively"
So I thought if I ran through a burning house,
   pulled a rabbit out a hat
Got a few foster kids, fed the poor, and ran up a
   tree to save a cat
Maybe America would notice me and see me for who
   I really am
I was on a mission for America without a self-
   proclaimed plan
See, America could care less if I could do
   without help
Trying to convince America, I didn't even
   convince myself
So scared of America's image of me, I didn't
   bother to look in the mirror

America is just like me, and I'm just as good as
    her
I remember as a kid I thought I could make *it*
    because I felt *it* inside
People said it, but I knew there was something
    different in my mind
I tried to fade the fact that art wasn't just in
    my life, but my life is art
This is me, whether you like it or not, America
I'm not a cop, but I can make people feel safer
I'm not a scientist, but I test words and make
    them real
I'm not a doctor, but somehow I cure emotions and
    make people feel
I'm not a lawyer, but I can advocate all sides of
    life, whether wrong or right
I'm not an executive, but I run a multi-idea
    business through sight
I'm not a teacher, but I can communicate concepts
    with a mental lesson plan
I'm not the president, but I can lead inspiration
    with a single hand
So, fuck you, America
'Cause today I decided I'm not *damn* afraid of ya
You can try to hold me back with your silly
    excuses
But only I know where my truth is
So if my race and gender is always going to be a
    problem
My degree is here, but this art will lead to my
    freedom
I know my ancestries will be happy with this
    self-affirmed change
I'm finally making it in America, even though I'm
    American made

About the Author

Live from Brooklyn, New York, in the 1980s—deep into the crack era, with immigration rising and hip-hop beginning—a poet was simultaneously birthed. Shari Valentina DeCastro, also known as MsQuoted, arose from childhood adversities to become a refined and skillful writer. At age twelve, an unruly encounter led her to ignite her talent, and this gift strengthened her throughout her life. This skill revealed its power to inspire the lives of others along her path.

MsQuoted also has a rich Haitian culture and family background that fuels her character and her determination to pursue her life as a poet. She is a graduate from Temple University, having attained a bachelor of arts in psychology. Her experiences and education worked concurrently to build a profound devotion to society. MsQuoted built a solid career serving children, volunteering her time in prisons, planning artistic events for the community, and counseling friends, families, and strangers for years. She is an advocate for the youth and uses her words to continuously uplift and move the change.

She knows her abilities as a writer, storyteller, and teacher will further her accomplishments as she continues to pursue her dreams and goals. She has received worthy praises regarding her writings. However, there is an abundance of success waiting at her fingertips, literally.

MsQuoted is more than just her name. It signifies her overall philosophy. Life is an uninterrupted quote. Therefore, keep reading!